1,000,000 Books

are available to read at

www.ForgottenBooks.com

Read online
Download PDF
Purchase in print

ISBN 978-1-5277-3880-5
PIBN 10885972

1 MONTH OF
FREE
READING

at

www.ForgottenBooks.com

By purchasing this book you are eligible for one month membership to ForgottenBooks.com, giving you unlimited access to our entire collection of over 1,000,000 titles via our web site and mobile apps.

To claim your free month visit:

www.forgottenbooks.com/free885972

English
Français
Deutsche
Italiano
Español
Português

www.forgottenbooks.com

Mythology Photography **Fiction**
Fishing Christianity **Art** Cooking
Essays Buddhism Freemasonry
Medicine **Biology** Music **Ancient
Egypt** Evolution Carpentry Physics
Dance Geology **Mathematics** Fitness
Shakespeare **Folklore** Yoga Marketing
Confidence Immortality Biographies
Poetry **Psychology** Witchcraft
Electronics Chemistry History **Law**
Accounting **Philosophy** Anthropology
Alchemy Drama Quantum Mechanics
Atheism Sexual Health **Ancient History**
Entrepreneurship Languages Sport
Paleontology Needlework Islam
Metaphysics Investment Archaeology
Parenting Statistics Criminology
Motivational

MEMOIRS

OF THE

SECRET SERVICES

OF

JOHN MACKY, Efq;

During the REIGNS of

King WILLIAM, Queen ANNE, and King GEORGE I.

INCLUDING, ALSO,

The true SECRET HISTORY of the Rife, Promotions, &c. of the *Englifh* and *Scots* No-BILITY; Officers, Civil, Military, Naval, and other Perfons of Diftinction, from the REVOLUTION. In their refpective CHARAC-TERS at large; drawn up by Mr. MACKY, purfuant to the Direction of Her ROYAL HIGHNESS the Princefs SOPHIA.

Publifhed from his Original Manufcript; As attefted by his SON

SPRING MACKY, Efq;

The SECOND EDITION.

L O N D O N:
Printed in the Year M.DCC.XXXIII.
(Price 5 s.)

ro 17/12/32

TO THE

PRINCE of WALES.

IT is humbly prefumed, that, there will not need any ftronger Motive to incite Your Royal Highnefs's Perufal of thefe Papers, than the Authority of Your moft Illuftrious Predeceffor, whofe Stamp they bear.

THE great Efteem which the Electrefs Dowager of *Hanover* had for Mr. *Macky*'s Services, is here apparent under Her own Hand.

A 2   ALL

DEDICATION.

ALL therefore that is farther neceſſary, is only to aſſure Your Royal Highneſs, that theſe CHARACTERS are faithfully printed from the Author's Original Manuſcript, and were drawn up by the Direction of the Princeſs SOPHIA, as is atteſted both by HIMSELF and his SON.

I am

Your ROYAL HIGHNESS's

Great *Ruſſel-ſtreet*,   moſt devoted.
Bloomsbury, Sept.
20th. 1732.-

              Humble Servant,

A. R.

TO THE

READER.

· *Sept.* 20th. 1732.

PRetty *near the Time thefe Papers were promifed the Publick they now appear.*

Moft of thefe Characters *are inferted by Bifhop* Burnet *in the* Second *and* Third *Volumes of the* Hiftory *of his* own Time, *which will not as yet fee the Light, for Reafons his Son* Thomas *could give, if he thought proper.*

It is evident from the Bifhop's WILL *, *That his whole Hiftory ought to have been publifhed above ten Years ago.*

* See Appendix, Numb. I.

The

To the READER.

The helping Hand, which the good Prelate
gave towards the Divorce, which, he says,
was intended between King CHARLES II.
and Queen Catharine, is sufficiently seen
in the Solutions of his Two Cases of Con-
science †. Why these anecdotes were omitted in the First Volume, his Son would do
well to inform us, since his Father desired
that his WORK might be printed faithfully as he left it, without adding, sup-
pressing, or altering it, in any Particular; for this (says the Editor) is my po-
sitive CHARGE and COMMAND.

As Truth is generally brought to Light
by Time; it is to be hoped that these
PAPERS, of Mr. Macky, will occasion
the speedy Publication of Bishop Burnet's
History.

VALE.

† See Appendix, Numb. II.

THE

THE
CONTENTS.

Mr.

TO THE

EDITOR.

SIR,

BEING *informed, that You are about to publish* CHA-RACTERS, &c. *written by Mr.* JOHN MACKY, *at the Desire of Her Royal Highness Princess* SOPHIA, *Electress Dowager of* Hanover ; *I think it becomes me, as his Son, to prevent any Falsities concerning him. Wherefore, I send you the inclosed* MEMORIAL, *of his own framing, which shows how faithful and*

A *active*

fhould land in *England* from the Coaft
of *Normandy*. He made fuch Hafte to
London, as to be there before King *James*
could reach *La Hogue*, the Place of Ren-
dezvous for his Army : And King *William* being in *Holland*, Mr. *Macky*'s Information was taken at my Lord *Sidney*'s
Office before the Earls of *Nottingham* and
Romney (then Lord *Sidney*) and Mr.
Johnftoun Secretary of State for *Scotland*.

The Information was of fuch Moment, and fo particular, that they did
not know what to think of it; my
Lord *Nottingham*, particularly, was very
doubtful and cold, till a Week after, that
my Lord *Portland* (to whom Mr. *Macky*
had alfo wrote) arrived from *Holland* with
the Confirmation of the whole : Whereupon a Fleet was immediately ordered
out from *Chatham*, under the Command
of Admiral *Ruffell*, to reinforce Admiral *Carter*, who burnt the *French* Fleet
in Sight of King *James* and his Army;
yet this Fleet had been too late, if a
ftrong

ſtrong Eaſterly Wind had not kept the *French* back for ſix Weeks.

· Mr. *Macky* alſo diſcovered Mr. *Harry Browne,* Brother to the Lord Viſcount *Montacute,* and Secretary of State to King *James; Francis Stafford,* Brother to the Earl of *Stafford,* and Gent. of the Bed-chamber to King *James ;* Colonel *Parker,* and Captain *Stow,* who were ſent over to prepare the Way for their King's Landing, and had them ſeized : As alſo above forty Officers, who were then raiſing Troops to make a Junction.

The Truth of theſe Services will be vouched by the Earl of *Nottingham,* and Secretary *Johnſtoun,* ſtill alive.

Mr. *Macky* neither asked nor received any Reward for theſe Services; but, on King *William's* Return from *Holland,* was appointed Inſpector of the Coaſt from *Harwich* to *Dover,* with a Salary, in order to prevent the treaſonable Correſpondence between *England* and *France,*

car-

carried on by Paffengers and Letters. He intercepted Mrs. *Aldridge* coming from St. *Germains*, with feventy Letters in a falfe Bottom of a Box with foul Linen; which Letters gave the firft Infight into the fecond Invafion intended from *Calais*, which terminated in an Affaffination. It was upon this Occafion that Mr. *Macky* wrote a Treatife called, *A View of the Court of St.* Germains, in order to open the Eyes of the People, in cafe the Defcent had been made ; of which Mr. *Richard Baldwin* the Printer fold Thirty Thoufand, 1696 *.

Mr. *Macky* alfo feized Captain *I a Rue*, coming directly from *France*, who was afterwards brought in as an Evidence in the Affaffination.

Thefe Services will be vouched by Secretary *Vernon* ftill alive.

* The Defign of this Piece was to fhew, The little Refpect King *James* had for thofe *Proteftants*, who followed his Fortunes into *France*.

By

By the Peace of *Refwick* the Communication with *France* being opened,
King *William* gave the Direction of the
Packet-boats from *Dover* to *France* and
Flanders to Mr. *Macky*; which however he could not have carried on, if he
had not then ma ried Sir *Thomas Spring's*
Sifter in *Suffolk*, whofe Portion went
entirely in building and fitting out five
new Packet-boats for that Service.

It would be tedious to mention the
feveral Letters and Perfons intercepted
by Mr. *Macky* during that fhort three
Years Peace ; I will only trouble you
with two memorable Paffages that happened, which, with all the reft, will be
vouched by Secretary *Vernon*, and Mr.
Ellis, then Under-Secretary to Lord
Jerfey, and ftill alive.

Mr. *Macky* received a Letter from my
Lord *Jerfey*, then Secretary of State, or-
dering him to attend the King at *Mar-*
A 4   *gate,*

Carney's Death, who made ufe of it purely to get a little Money.

However, the Scheme was fo plaufible, and fo eafy to be put in Execution, that it occafioned a Bill being brought into Parliament for purchafing Ground for fortifying *Chatham*, and the Paffe; on the River *Medway*, which were all unguarded before, and no Troops quartered within two Days Journey.

There were two Women that were permitted to go to St. *Germain*'s with Gloves, and other Trinkets, which the Family wanted from *England*, who were very ufeful in giving an Account of thofe Lords and Gentlemen who privately waited on King *James* from *England*, which they never failed of, and were entertained by Mr. *Macky*, as is well known to Secretary *Vernon*.

King

King *William* repofed fuch an entire
Confidence in Mr. *Macky*, that all the
private Expreffes between his Majefty
and Lord *Portland*, during the *Partition
Treaty* went thro' Mr. *Macky*'s Hands,
without paffing through either the *Englifh*
or *French* Poft-houfes; and Mr. *Macky*
kept a Servant on purpofe to ride between
Dover and *Paris* with thefe Expreffes,
which is very well known to Secretary
Vernon, and Mr. *D'Olonne.*

At King *William*'s Death a new War
breaking out, and the *Communication* with
France confequently fhut, Mr *Macky*'s Pac‑
quet-boats were laid afide, and all the Money they coft loft, and there was too good
an Underftanding between the Courts of
St. James's, and *St. Germain's*, for himfelf
to expect any Thing, he therefore accepted
of a Commiffion to go to look after an
Eftate in the Ifland of *Zant*, in the Domi-
nion of *Venice*; a Quarter of which be-
longed to him by Right of his Wife, and
another

another Quarter Sir *Samuel Dashwood,* and Sir *John Cordell,* the Executors, gave him for his Trouble. He took *Hanover,* and the other Courts of *Germany* in his Way, and at the Princess *Sophia's* Defire, gave her the CHARACTERS of the great Men of *England* and *Scotland,* which Service, with many others, her Royal Highnefs hath Acknowledged by Letters, which Mr. *Macky* ftill hath by him *.

By the Battle of *Ramellies,* and the taking of *Oftend,* all *Flanders* being reduced, the Lord *Godolphin* fent Mr. *Macky* over to fettle an Intercourfe of Letters directly between *England* and thefe Countries, and gave him the Direction of the Pacquet-Boats to *Oftend,* with Inftructions to have a watchful Eye over the Naval Preparations from Time to Time at *Dunkirk,* which was eafy to be done

---

* See the *Appendix,* Numb. III. and IV.

from

from *Oſtend,* moſt of the *Dunkirkers* being Navigated by *Oſtenders.*

The *Dunkirkers* had Advice from *Holland,* of a very rich Fleet bound from
thence to *Topſham* in the Weſt of *England,* under Convoy of two *Dutch* Men
of War to the *Downs,* and two *Engliſh*
Men of War from the *Downs* to *Topſham;*
whereupon they fitted out eight ſmall
Frigates to intercept them, and to wait
for them off of *Dungenneſs.* Mr. *Macky*
had Advice of this the very Tide they
ſailed, and as the *Topſham* Fleet was paſſing by the *South* Foreland, under the
Command of Commadore *Moody,* Mr.
Macky ſent a Boat off with the Letter,
adviſing the Commadore to ſtop his
Fleet, till he ſent his ſmalleſt Frigate to
reconnoitre, which accordingly he did, and
ſaw the eight Sail lying ſnug under the
Neſs; upon which the Fleet returned
into the *Downs,* or had been every Ship
taken. This is very well known to Captain *Moody* ſtill alive.

Mr.

Mr. *Macky* had another time Advice of fix Frigates failing from *Dunkirk* to cruife upon our *Northern* Traders off of the Banks of *Tarmouth*; he fent this Letter to Sir *Thomas Hardy* then Commadore in the *Downs*, who had my Lord *Duffus* at Dinner with him, and who was then ordered to fail Northward in the Advice Man of War: His Lordfhip fell in with thefe fix Frigates, exactly conform to Mr. *Macky*'s Information, and after a gallant Defence, was taken by them and carried into *Dunkirk* This will be vouched by Sir *Thomas Hardy* ftill alive.

In the Year 1708, when the great Armament was making at *Dunkirk*, which the *Dunkirkers* themfelves did not know what it was for, Mr. *Macky* fent an Inhabitant of the Country with a *French* Pafs, under pretence of making up fome old Accompts with *Pigault*, a Merchant in *Calais*, to which *Dunkirk* was his Road; he very luckily fell in with

with the Troops on their March, that
were defigned for this Expedition, and
foon found they were bound for *Scotland*; he brought Mr. *Macky* the Name
of every Battalion and every Ship, which
Mr. *Macky* immediately tranfmitted to
my Lord *Sunderland* then Secretary of
State. Lord *Sunderland* fent Mr. *Macky*'s Letter to the Lords of the Admiralty,
who were of Opinion, that it was a Feint
of *France*, to ftop Sir *John Leake*'s failing
with the Tranfports to *Portugal*, who were
then ready, and not a real Defign of landing; but,in four Days after Mr. *Macky* went
Poft to *London*, with the certain Advice,
that the *Pretender* was himfelf in Perfon
arrived at *Dunkirk*, in order to imbark;
notwithftanding which Sir *John Leake* was
ordered to proceed, and Sir *George Byng*
with a Squadron was ordered out to
look after him. What was the Reafon,
I cannot tell; but the Miniftry were as
unwilling to believe this Defcent, as that
of *La Hogue*. My Lord *Sunderland* and
his Secretary Mr. *Hopkins* being dead, I
muft

muft appeal to Sir *Stafford Fairborne*, who was then one of the Lords of the Admiralty, and to Sir *Thomas Franckland* Poftmafter General, for the Veracity of this.

But the fatal Information which was Mr. *Macky*'s Ruin, and which he hath never been able to retrieve, was a Letter he received from *Calais*, that an *Englifh* Gentleman arrived there that Morning in a Boat directly from the River *Thames*; that he took Poft immediately for *Paris*; and that the Boat waited his Return. Mr. *Macky* fent this Account to my Lord *Bolingbroke*, then Secretary of State; who by his Secretary Mr. *Tilfon* defired him to fay nothing of it, but to look out for his Return: Accordingly Mr. *Macky* employed all his People between the *Forelands*, by which the Boat muft pafs to return, to look out for her, and at laft had Advice, that fhe landed at *Deal* three Perfons with my Lord *Bolingbroke*'s Pafs. Mr. *Macky* upon this Advice

made

made hafte to *Canterbury*, through which
they muft pafs, and to his Surprize
found the Gentleman by the Name of
Matthews to be his old Acquaintance
Mr. *Prior*, and Monfieur *Menager*, and
the *Abbé Gautier*.

Mr. *Macky* difpatched an Exprefs that
Night to the Duke of *Marlborough*, then
at the Siege of *Bouchain*, with this important News; but whether his Grace
could not believe, that the Miniftry
would make fuch a Step without him,
Mr. *Macky's* Letter was expofed, and a
Copy of it fent by Mr. *Watkins* to Lord
Bolingbroke. Mr *Macky* alfo took Horfe
for *Tunbridge*, and acquainted the Bifhop
of *Winchefter* and Admiral *Aylmer* with
the Matter, that they might inform my
Lord *Sunderland*. he alarms Count *Gal-
las* and Mr. *Iftingham*; and Mr. *Macky*
being found to be the Perfon with all
the Train that fprung the Mine, it
brought down the Indignation of the
Miniftry furioufly upon him. My Lord

b   *Boling-*

Bolingbroke threatned to hang him for keeping a Correſpondence with *France*. The Earl of *Oxford* ordered the Poſt-maſters to ſend his Contract for the Pacquet-Boats to the Attorney-General for his Opinion in Point of Law; his Creditors were hounded out upon him; he was thrown into Priſon, and there he lay at the King's Acceſſion to the Throne.

When he obtained his Liberty, all the good Employments being given away, and his Pacquet-Boats at *Dover* branched out into particular Contracts for five Years, of which but half a Year was expired, my Lord *Townſhend* Secretary of State adviſed Mr. *Macky* to accept of the Pacquet-Boats to *Dublin*, and that they would make them worth his while: He went to *Ireland*, built Packet-Boats at a great Expence, and ran himſelf in Debt; for the Income of theſe Boats never anſwered the Expence. All which hath been laid
before

before the Secretaries of State, and Lords of the Treasury, without Relief; and Mr. *Macky*, after thirty Years Service, is now in a worse Condition than ever.

N. B. *This* MEMORIAL *had so happy an Effect, that Mr.* Macky *was sent Abroad ; where the Services he performed were so considerable,* † *that even after they were over, Sir* Robert Walpole *continued to supply him, in so generous a manner, as rendered the close of his Life much more easy to him than the former Part had been. He died at* Rotterdam, *in the Year* 1726, *and was there buried.*

A Person of the first Rank, hearing that these Papers, of Mr. *Macky*, were in the Press, has been pleased to communicate to us a Copy of his *View of the*

---

† Particularly in detecting the Correspondence of the late Bishop of *Rochester.*

B 2   *Court*

Court of St. German *, mentioned in the foregoing *Memorial*. There having been *Thirty Thousand of them sold*, as Mr. *Macky* therein declares; and he laying no small Stress upon the good Effects which that *Tract* produced, we thought it would be acceptable to every Reader to have the Perusal of so remarkable a Piece, which Mr. *Macky* thus introduces, *viz.*

" The Ages to come, (*says he*) will
" hardly believe, that in *England* there
" should be found one single *Protestant*
" *Jacobite*, at this time of Day: And
" the Reformed Nations *Abroad*, are at
" a Loss what to make of that unac-
" countable Species of Men.

" When most of the *Roman Catholick*
" Princes have heartily embraced the late

* The whole Title runs thus. *A View of the Court of* St. *Germain,* from the Year 1690, to 1695, *with an Account of the Entertainment* Protestants *meet with there, directed to the Malecontent Protestants of* England.

" Re-

" Revolution in *Britain,* as the laſt
" Effort for the Common Liberty of *Eu-*
" *rope,* and have entered into the ſtrict-
" eſt Alliance, with thoſe of an oppo-
" ſite Religion to ſupport it. It looks
" like a Dream to meet with any *Engliſh*
" Proteſtant in an Intereſt contradicto-
" ry to, not only the Publick Liberty of
" their Country, but to the Religion
" they profeſs.

" It was indeed no great Wonder
" that King *James* made all the Steps
" poſſible towards the Change of a Re-
" ligion, in his Opinion, Heretical; at
" a time when he was upon the Throne,
" and backed with all the promiſing
" Supports of Regal Power, yet even
" then he thought himſelf obliged to
" keep ſome Meaſures with his Pro-
" teſtant Subjects, and inſtead of a to-
" tal Rupture with them, endeavoured
" to lull them aſleep, under the ſpecious
" Pretence of *Liberty* of *Conſcience,* till

" all

" all his Engines were ready to give the
" fatal Blow.

" But now, that he has fallen under
" Circumftances, which one would
" think fhould much more than ever
" oblige him to affume a New, at leaft
" keep on the Old Mask: Upon the
" quite contrary fince he went to *France*;
" he has taken all the Pains imaginable
" to let the World know his inveterate
" Averfion to all thofe of the Reformed
" Religion, tho' ever fo much his
" Friends; and at the fame time has
" given us the moft authentick Demon-
" ftration of his firm Defign, never to
" allow any thereof his Favour, nor
" owe his Reftoration to any but *Roman*
" *Catholicks.* All which will appear by
" the following Account of his Carri-
" age towards thofe few *Proteftants* who
" have followed his finking Fortunes
" the length of St. *Germain.*

A

A View of the COURT *of* Saint Germain, *Addreffed to the* Malecontent Proteftants *of* England.

THERE being already fo many Volumes written, to fhew the Lawfulnefs of the late *Revolution,* it is fuperfluous, it feems, to make any farther Attempt on the fame Subject: For if you have fhut your Eyes againft the ftrong Arguments and convincing Proofs made ufe of in thofe Books, who can flatter himfelf, that he fhall be able to cure you of your wilful Blindnefs ? However, I hope, this plain Account which I make bold to direct to you, will not prove altogether ufelefs, for when I confider your Party, I think

I

I may reafonably believe that it is m
up of fome good and honeft Men, t
mifguided by a tender Confcience, a
of fome felf-interefted Perfons, who l
ing not able to obtain the Preferme
they expected, haye turned *Jacobites*,
hopes to advance their Fortune by a
cond Revolution. But give me leave
tell you farther, that after an impar
Enquiry into the Life and Converfat
of your Party, I have all the Reafons
the World to conclude, that the Nu
ber of the *Confcientious Jacobites* I h:
fpoken of, muft be very few, and t
the greateft part of you, are hurried av
by the imaginary Hopes I have hin
at; therefore if I can convince you, t
you have no reafon to flatter your felv
to obtain any Reward or Preferme
under King JAMES, no, not if he fhoi
be reftored by your Means, I hope foi
of you will open your Eyes to yc
own Intereft, and forfake a Prince frc
whom you cannot expect any grate
Return.

I will not recal to your Minds his Behaviour while he was on the Throne of *England*, I suppose no body has forgot, that *no Proteſtants* were welcome to him, but such as would promiſe to betray the Liberties of their Country to *Popery*, and *Arbitrary Power*; neither ſhall I mention how ſeverely he uſed the Proteſtants of *Ireland* in 1689; you would be apt to ſay, That being in *Popiſh Hands*, he could not avoid it, but I intend only to give you *a ſhort View of his Court at St.* Germain, and an Account of the Entertainment the *Proteſtants* of your *Party* have met there: For if a Prince in his Circumſtances, whoſe Intereſt it ought to be to court Proteſtants, cannot conceal for a time the Hatred he has for them, what Treatment can you expect from him, when he is re-inthroned, and ſupported by the Power of *France*.

King

King *James* retiring into *France* after his Defeat at the *Boyne*, left the Administration of his Affairs in *Ireland* to my Lord *Tyrconnel*, and in *Scotland* the Colonels *Buchan* and *Cannan*, and the *French* King having appointed St. *Germain en Laye* for his Reception, he there began to form a Court in the Year 1690, and his Houshold was constituted, as follows.

The Duke of *Powis*, Lord Chamberlain.

Colonel *Porter*, Vice Chamberlain.

Colonel *Skelton*, Comptroller.

The Earl of *Dunbarton* and *Abercorn*, Lords of the Bed-chamber.

Captains, *Macdonald*, *Peadles*, *Stafford*, and *Trevanian*, Grooms of the Bed-Chamber.

The

The two *Sheldons*, Esquires.

Fergus Graham, Privy-Purse.

Sir *John Sparrow*, Board of Green-Cloth, and Mr. *Strickland*, Vice Chamberlain to the Queen.

The Officers of State were as follows,

MR. *Brown* (Brother to my Lord *Montague Brown*, and sometime Commissioner of the Customs) Secretary of State for *England*.

Father *Innes*, President of the *Scots* College at *Paris*, Secretary of State for *Scotland*.

Sir *Richard Neagle*, Secretary of State for *Ireland*.

To

To thefe were added as a Junto, Mr. *Caryl*, the Queen's Secretary, and Mr. *Stafford*, formerly Envoy at the Court of *Spain*, whom the King called together as a Privy-Council, to advife with upon all Emergencies: The Earl of *Melfort*, Prime Minifter of State, being fent to *Rome*, fometime before, partly to Negotiate King *James's* Affairs at the Pope's Court, and partly to remove him from the Jealoufies of the *Irifh*, who, at that Time, wholly monopolized this Prince's Ear and Favour.

Thus things continued for a while, but *Ireland* being reduced fometime after, and the *Scottifh Highlanders* fubmitting, the Court of St. *Germain* was every Day thronged with Gentlemen from thofe Kingdoms, as well as from *England*; and then a Proteftant Party began to diftinguifh themfelves, and endeavoured to make an Appearance at that Court.

The

The firſt conſiderable Step they took,
was to deſire a Chapel of King *James*,
or the Exerciſe of their Worſhip ac-
ording to the Church of *England*, and
propoſed Dr. *Granville*, Brother to the
Earl of *Bath*, formerly Dean of *Durham*,
is a fit Perſon to be their Chaplain ;
they urged the great Encouragement,
ſuch a Toleration would give to his Ad-
herents in *England*, and what Satisfaction
it would be to ſuch *Proteſtants* as followed him; but tho' common Policy,
and his Circumſtances made every Body
believe that this Requeſt would be eaſily
granted, yet it was poſitively denied, and
Dr. *Granville* obliged not only to retire
from Court, but alſo from the Town
of St. *Germain*, to avoid the daily In-
ſults of the Prieſts, and the dreaded
Conſequences of the Jealouſies with which
they poſſeſſed King *James*'s Court againſt
him. Dr. *Gordon*, a Biſhop of *Scotland*,
the only *Proteſtant* Divine then there,
met with a yet worſe Treatment than
Dr.

mirted to the *Baſtile*. Thus was this Lord Chief Juſtice, for no other Reaſon, but his adhering to a *Proteſtant* Intereſt, excluded from all Share of Management of Affairs in King *James*'s Court, tho'his Capacity and Sufferings were ſufficient in the Eyes of all reaſonable Men; to have intitled him to a Share in that Prince's Favour and Secrets. If my Lord Chief Juſtice *Herbert* was ſo uſed, I would fain know upon what Ground any of our *Jacobites* would flatter themſelves of a better Treatment.

Mr. *Cockburn* of *Lanton*, in the Kingdom of *Scotland*, was the next *Proteſtant* who had Merit and Favour enough to pretend to a Share in the Management of King *James*'s Affairs. This Gentleman having followed him into *Ireland*, was taken at Sea, after the Battle of the *Boyne*, and brought Priſoner to *London* : But a Propoſal being made of exchanging him for Captain *Saintloe*, then Priſoner in *France*, he was enlarged, and during his
Abode

.bode here, did so ingratiate himself
ith the most considerable of the dis-
fected Protestants, ~~what~~ he was recom-
ended by them to King *James*, as a
erson fit to serve him in the Affairs of
eatest Trust.   He was no sooner ar-
ved at St. *Germain*, than he told that
rince, his Friends in *England* thought
at my Lord *Melfort*, who was then
turned from *Rome*, was a great Grie-
ance, and ought to be laid aside ; and
at the only Way for the King to pre-
ire the good Opinion of his Subjects
ı *Britain*, and reconcile them to him,
as to put the Management of his Affairs
ıto *Protestant Hands*.   This prudent
dvice of the disaffected *Protestants* of
ngland, or of Mr. *Cockburn*, had an
ffect quite contrary to what they ex-
ected; King *James* took it so ill, that
. a few Days after, an Order was pro-
ıred from the *French* Court, command-
g him to depart *France* under severe
nalties, being too much a Friend to
e *English* Interest ; Mr. *Cockburn* was

C

forced

in the Night, where they thrust him
in.

Nor was Colonel *Cannan* better used,
than my Lord *Dumferling* : This Gentleman commanded as General over
King *James's* Army in *Scotland*, and
served him with so much Faithfulness,
that every Body thought he would be
preferred to a great Command, upon
his arrival at St. *Germain* ; but he po-
sitively refusing to abandon the *little Religion he had*, which was *Protestant*, was
reduced to the scandalous Allowance of
Half a Crown a Day, whilst *Papists*, who
had served under him, were advanced to
good Posts.   This unhappy Gentleman
finding himself thus neglected, fell Sick
through Grief and Want, and died ; having taken the Sacrament from the
Hands of Dr. *Granville*, three Days before his Death ; but the Priests, who
were always buzzing about him, took
the Opportunity of his being speechless,
to thrust a Wafer down his Throat, and
gave

gave out that he died a *Papist*, and by this Means got him the Favour of Burial, which his Corps had else been excluded from, as well as my Lord *Dumferling*'s. If the Sufferings and great Merits of these two Gentlemen, have not been able to molify King *James*'s Heart, and to obtain from him any generous Returns, I would fain know upon what Foundation are grounded the great Hopes of our Grumblers, seeing the most Part of them have not had Courage enough to follow that Prince, and have for aught we see, no other Qualifications to recommend them, but their bare *Jacobitism*.

However, if the Examples I have already exposed to your View, are not sufficient to convince you, that as long as you are *Protestants*, and *English* Men, you are to expect no Share in King *James*'s Favour; I will produce some others, which I am sure, will open your Eyes, unless you are bound by an Oath

C 3   to

to continue always Blind. I fhall begin
with Sir *James Montgomery*.

This Gentleman left no Stone un-
turned to re-eftablifh King *James* in *Scotland*, by the fame Parliament, that declared him to have forfeited his Right :
He was afterwards, for feveral Years, his
moft active Minifter in *England*, drew
up and publifhed Declarations for him,
at the Time of his defigned Defcent from
La Hogue, and after the Mifcarriage of
That ; wrote *Britain's juft Complaints* ;
was his Weekly *News-writer*, and *Project
Drawer* ; yet this very Sir *James Montgomery*, who had done fuch great Things,
and run fuch Hazards for him, being
obliged to fly to *France*, after making
his Efcape from the Meffenger's Houfe,
could not obtain, by reafon of his being
a *Proteftant*, any Share of that Prince's
Favour ; was Brow-beaten from the
Court by Priefts, daily upbraided with
having been once in the Prince of
Orange's Intereft, and at laft obliged to
retire

retire to *Paris,* where he died with the melancholy Reflections of the miferable State he had brought himfelf into.

The Earl of *Lauderdale,* tho' a Papift, met with no better Fate than Sir *James.* His Lady being a *Proteftant,* and he an Enemy to the violent Meafures of the Court, was judged to be a fufficient Reafon for excluding him from any Share in the Government : So natural it is for all Bigots to hate every Body that will not go their Height of Violence. This Gentleman heartily advifed King *James* to put his Affairs into *Proteftant* Hands, and recommended the Earl of *Clarendon,* and the Non-juring Bifhops in *England,* and the Lords *Home, Southesk,* and *Sinclair* in *Scotland,* as the fitteft Perfons to ferve him; but his Advice was fo ill taken, that he had his Lady fent to *England,* not to return any more; was himfelf forbid the Court, and reduced to a Penfion of one Hundred Piftoles *per Annum :* He retired to *Paris,* and fee-

ing

xl *The* SECRET SERVICES

ing no probability of his Master's changing his Measures, died of Grief. One would have thought that his Brother, Mr. *Alexander Maitland*, who on several Occasions had behaved himself very bravely in that Prince's Service, should have been preferred by him, yet he met with such an Entertainment, that wanting Bread there, he was very glad to come to *England*, and make his Peace with the Government, whose Service he had deserted, having once had a Command in the *Scots Guards*, under King *William*.

Sir *Andrew Forrester*, is another great Instance of King *James*'s Aversion to Protestants: This Gentleman served, with all imaginable Zeal, that Prince's Interest when a Subject, and was the devoted Creature of his most Arbitrary Commands, when a King; he suffered Imprisonment in the *Tower* for him, at the time of his designed Descent, and yet, notwithstanding all this, and the great
Expe-

Experience he had in *Scottish Affairs*, he could never obtain any Share in that Prince's Confidence: When he came to St. *Germain*, all his Merits, Sufferings, and the good Character he had in both Kingdoms, were not enough to counter-balance the Objection of being a *Protestant*, and therefore by no means to be intrusted; so that after some time, attending as a Cypher, he was rewarded with a Pass to return to *England*, for they had, there, no Occasion for him.

Sir *Theophilus Oglethorp*, who by his Capacity as well as Services, was encouraged to go over, and offer his Assistance, met with Sir *Andrew Forrester's* Fate, on account of his Religion, and was so unkindly used, that he was very glad to get home to Old *England* again, where it is expected he will stir no more.

Mr. *Fergus Graham* was the only Protestant Gentleman in King *James's* Family; but as soon as they saw that my
Lord

Lord *Preston,* and Colonel *Graham* his
Brother, who ventured fo much for
that Prince, could do them no more
Service in *England,* he was difcharged
for no other Reafon, but that they
thought a *Proteftant* a Blemifh in their
Houfhold.

Nor was Sir *William Sharp* better ufed,
altho' he pretended to come over upon
the Act of Parliament in *Scotland,* to
fave his Eftate. The Entertainment
he had at St. *Germain,* before he came
away, is very well known. The Penfion he had whilft King *James*'s Army in
Scotland kept up, was taken from him,
and he fell under diftruft, with *Melfort*
and *Innes,* and Contempt at Court,
which will appear to all reafonable Men
a fufficient Motive for his coming away.

But the ufage of Dr. *Cockburn* a *Scottifh* Divine, is beyond any thing that
can be imagined. This Gentleman was
banifhed *Scotland* for his Practices againft
the

e Government, and afterwards being
urged to leave *England*, for writing
empties, thought himself secure of a
.... at St. *Germain*, if not of a Re-
.... for his Services; but instead of
.... with the daily importunities
.... to make him abandon his
.... and these Endeavours proving
.... represented him as a
.... Enemy, and got him sent
into *France*. He now lives in Exile in
.... twixt *Britain* and *France*.

.... Treaty of the Union,
....
....
....
....
....
....
....
....
....
....
....
Queen ....

woman declining to comply with, was neglected, and dying foon after, was refufed Burial, till her Father, Mr. *Rigby* of *Covent-Garden*, as a mighty Favour, and at great Charges, obtained leave from the Court of St. *Germain*, to have her Body brought over into *England*, and buried in his Parifh Church.

If thefe Examples are not fufficient to convince our *Jacobites*, or if they que-ftion the Truth of them, for really I muft own, that they are almoft incre-dible; I defire them to confult the young Lord *Kenmure*, Mr. *Louthian*, Captains *Murray, Dalzel, Macgil, Maclean, Field-ing*, Mr. *Charles Kinnard*, and feveral hundreds more, now *in*, and *about Lon-don*, who are lately come from St. *Ger-main*, and they will tell you, that the only Reafon why they left that Court, was, becaufe they could not have Bread, except they would change their Religi-on, and therefore they rather chofe to run the Hazard of Imprifonment, by return-ing

ing to *England*, than ftay, and ftarve in *France*.

Many Inftances more might be given, to fhew King *James's* hatred to every thing, that bears the ˙ Name of *Proteftant*; but if what has already been faid, is not fufficient, fure I am, that more would be to no purpofe : What *Proteftant* has he ever fo much as *feemed* to truft, fince he has been in *France*? I know that my Lord *Middleton* muft be excepted, for indeed King *James* has a feeming Truft in him. There is no Man who has been at St. *Germain*, but muft needs perceive, that he is not chief Minifter, as *Melfort* was, nor manages Affairs betwixt *Verfailles* and St. *Germain*; That being done by *Innes* and *Porter* : He is but feldom called to Council, and the *French* Court has never depended upon his Correfpondence, fince the Difappointment they received by our Fleets going into the *Streights*.

I

The Education of the Prince of *Wales*, whom no body doubts he defigns his Succeffor, is another Inftance of his irreconcileable Antipathy to the *Proteftant* Religion, and *Englifh* Liberties: One would have thought, that Intereft, as well as Policy, would have made him educate his Child a *Proteftant*, or at leaft cblige him to put *Proteftants* about him, of unqueftioned Reputation, to inftruct him in the ways of pleafing the People; but inftead of that, Dr. *Beefton*, a famous and violent Papift, was made his Preceptor, and none but Popifh Servants are allowed to be about him; fo that he can imbibe nothing but what is for the Intereft of *Rome*, and Deftruction of *England*.

Can People be fo mad as to expect good Terms from a Prince, who not only thus treats his *Proteftant* Subjects, who have followed him in his Misfortune, but alfo whofe Religion lays him under

under a Neceffity of doing it? Could greater Obligations be laid upon any Prince, than were upon him, by the Church of *England*, when a Subject? Her Intereft faved him from being profecuted for the Popifh Plot, excluded from the Succeffion to the *Englifh* Throne, and prevented his being dethroned by the Duke of *Monmouth*; yet all thefe *Obligations*, nor his *Coronation Oath*, would not hinder him from invading the *Proteftant* Religion in general, but more particularly the Liberties of the Church of *England*.

Yet perhaps fome will object againft what I have faid, that from the Entertainment *Proteftants* meet with at St. *Germain*, it is not reafonable to conclude, that King *James* bears ftill fuch an Averfion to our Religion and Liberties: For being himfelf but a *Refugeé* in *France*, and having nothing to live upon but the Penfion the *French* King allows him, it is not in his Power to reward

thofe

thofe *Proteflants* who have followed him,
even not to carefs them; and therefore
we ought rather to perufe the *Declara-*
tions he has put out fince his being in
France, for therein we fhall find undeni-
able Proofs, that his Misfortunes have
much altered his Mind. *Read* (will our
Jacobites fay) the *Declaration* he publifhed upon his intended Defcent from
La Hogue, and obferve what Promifes
he makes, both in relation to our Religion and our Liberties, the Sincerity
whereof, you have no manner of Pretence to queftion; for then, thinking
himfelf fure of his Game, nothing could
oblige him to difguife the true Sentiments of his Heart.

This is fomewhat indeed, Gentlemen,
and were the thing as you fay, I would
agree with you, but give me leave to
tell you, that it is a great Queftion,
whether the *Declaration* you fpeak of,
which was printed at *London,* did really contain King *James's* Sentiments;
but

but whether it was his own Declaration, or Sir *James Montgomery's*, is not a Pin Matter; for his Majesty publickly disowned it in a *Memorial* to the *Pope*, upon his return to *Paris*; and it has been acknowledged in a *Jacobite* Pamphlet, called, *An Anſwer to Dr.* Welwood*'s Anſwer, to King* James*'s Declaration*; That the same was framed without his Knowledge, and againſt his Inclination.

I have told you in the Beginning of this Diſcourſe, that I believe there are among you ſome conſcientious Men, and to thoſe I ſhall not ſay any Thing at this Time, but to ſuch as are angry with the *preſent Government* (as I know many among you are) merely becauſe you cannot have any Employment under it, and who think without any farther Examination, to better their Condition by a *Second* Revolution : I will ſay, they ought to conſider, that King *James's* Popiſh Friends, muſt be all provided for firſt of all ; and pray then

what

what will remain for you? For, as to Penſions, I think you are not ſo mad as to flatter your ſelves with ſuch imaginary Hopes, for the *French* Army that brings King *James* over, muſt be paid; alſo the vaſt Charges of the *Iriſh* War, and the Maintenance of King *James* reimburſed, before your beloved Prince can be in a Condition to expreſs his Favour to you. Perhaps you will ſay, that the *Trench* King is too much a Gentleman, to demand any ſuch Thing, but I do not know what ſhould give you ſuch a Noble Idea of his Generoſity; tho' ſuppoſing his Temper to be ſuch, this War will ſo much drain his *Exchequer*, that Neceſſity will force him to demand what is ſo juſtly owing to him, and who ſhall be able to diſpute his Bill of Charges? Nay, will King *James* be able to ſatisfy him? I do not know, but this I am ſure of, that as long as you profeſs the *Proteſtant* Religion, you cannot expect to be more favourably treated than his preſent Followers.

Some

Some others among you are Difaffect-
ed, becaufe, as they fay, without the Reftoration of King *James,* a *Proteftant* War
will be intailed on the Nation; and becaufe our Treafure is exhaufted by Taxes,
and our Blood expended beyond Sea,
which the Nation cannot long bear.

To thefe Gentlemen, I muft anfwer;

1. That they are much miftaken ; for
the bringing in King *James,* which they
think will put an end to thefe Troubles,
would infallibly remove the *Seat* of *War*
from *Flanders* into *England* : For it is
unreafonable to fuppofe, that fo many
Noblemen and Gentlemen as are engaged in King *William's* Caufe, will
tamely fubmit; or, that his Majefty,
whofe Intereft in *Europe* is fo very great,
will either inglorioufly abandon his
Throne, or want Foreign Affiftance to
fupport him in it.

2. King

2. King *James* and the *French* King are both old, and upon the Change of a Governour in *France*, we may reafonably expect change of Meafures; for as to the Prince of *Wales*, his Intereft ftands or falls, with that of his (*fuppofed*) Father; but, after all, is it reafonable to believe that the *French*, or any other Nation, will live in perpetual War with us, meerly for the Sake of a Prince, who pretends to be deprived of his Rights? There are very few *Knight-Errants* in this Age, or at leaft, fure I am, that no Nation is actuated by their Principles, and we fee the *French* already offer to forfake Him.

3. I grant, our Taxes are greater than ever our Nation paid; yet they are not fo heavy, but that we can hold it out many Years at this Rate. In fhort, whatever they be, I believe there is no good Man but will rather hazard his Perfon to keep the Enemy abroad, than
fee

fee a *French* and *Irish* Army in the Bowels of our own Country, deftroying our Subftance, burning our Habitations, and committing the Barbarities which they practiced in the *Palatinate* : For certainly by one Month's Ravage of this Nature, we fhould lofe more Blood and Treafure, than can probably be fpent to bring the War to an Honourable and Happy Conclufion.

That happy Moment is not perhaps fo far off as fome People imagine; for whofoever will caft his Eyes on the prefent Pofture of Affairs in *Europe*, muft needs conclude, that the *French* cannot hold it out much longer.

Here ends Mr. *Macky*'s View of the Court of St. *Germain*.

I fhall clofe thefe Papers with a *Second* Letter which I have received from his Son, *viz.*

To

To the EDITOR.

SIR,

THE Memorial *was framed the* Year *after Lord* Sunderland's *Death,* (1723) *but I cannot certainly tell for whom.* My Father's *Honour, and* Your *Satisfaction, were strong Motives to have exhibited every Particular of his* late *important Services; but I assure* You, *that the very mentioning of them, immediately discovers the Principal Actors; and may prove their utter Ruin.* You know Secret Services, *too recent, are not to be exposed: and I have sent* You *what I am sure* You *must think very valuable, and chiefly,* I protest, *with a View to serve* You. *All I can say is,* I *throw my self upon* Your *Friendship, and am,*

SIR,

Your very humble Servant,

Portsmouth,
12th Sept.
1732.

SPRING MACKY.

CHA-

CHARACTERS

OF THE

COURT

OF

GREAT BRITAIN.

His Royal Highnefs, Prince
George, Husband to Queen
Anne, and Lord High Admi-
ral of *England*,

IS Brother to the late King of *Den-*
mark, and Uncle to the prefent, was
hofen by King *Charles* the Second to
be Husband to his Niece, the Princefs
B   Anne;

Anne ; becaufe, having no Dominions of his own to gratify, he would have nothing elfe in View, but the Intereft of *England*.

In the Reign of King *Charles* the Second, having but little *Englifh*, and being naturally Modeft, he made no confiderable Figure, nor in the Reign of King *James*, till the Increafe of *Popery* alarming the whole Nation, he concurred with the reft of the *Proteftant* Nobility for the bringing over the Prince of *Orange*, and with his Princefs left the Court to join that Party.

During all King *William's* Reign, he never entered into the Adminiftration, yet came always to Parliament regularly, and often to Court ; diverted himfell with Hunting, and never openly declared himfelf of any Party.

· On the Queen's Acceffion to the Crown, he was made Lord High-Admira mind of *England*, and Warden of the *Cinque-Ports*. He is a Prince of a familiar, easy Disposition, with a good, sound Understanding, not much given to showing it: A great Lover of the *Church of England*, ... comes to *Lechery*: This he sometimes shews, by his Vote in the House of Peers; otherwise he doth not much meddle with Affairs out of his Office.

He is very fat, loves News, his Bottle, and the Queen, by whom he hath had many Children, but none alive. He hath neither many Friends nor Enemies in *England*. On the Queen's Accession to the Throne, he was toward Fifty Years old.

John Churchill, Duke of *Marl-borough*, Captain-General,

IS Son to Sir *Winston Churchill*, of a good Family. The Duke of *York's* Love for his Sister (by whom he had the Duke of *Berwick*, and other Children) first brought him to Court; and the Beauty of his own Person, and his good Address, so gained on the Dutchess of *Cleveland* (then Mistress to King *Charles* the Second) that she effectually established him there.

When the Duke of *York* was sent to *Scotland*, he was of his Family, and was there made a Lord, by the Title of Lord *Aymouth*; and, on that Prince's coming to the Throne, created a Baron of *England*, by the Title of Lord *Churchill*. He continued one of King *James's* chief Favourites all that Prince's Reign; was of his Council, and a Major-General of

his

his Army : But the great Progrefs of *Popery* fhocked him. His Love to his Country counter-balanced all King *James's* Favours, and drew him from that Prince's Perfon, to the Intereft of his Country ; which he handfomely expreffed in a Letter he fent to his Majefty, † giving much the fame Reafon that *Brutus* did for joining againft *Cæfar*.

He was the great Inftrument of bringing over the Army to the Prince of *Orange*; and, to the Admiration of every body, with a Handful of Men, reduced *Cork* and *King fale* in *Ireland*, with their numerous Garrifons, to King *William's* Obedience : And on his Acceffion to the Throne, was made Earl of *Marlborough*, and General of his Forces ; in which Poft he ferved alfo in *Flanders*, with univerfal Applaufe. On fome Difference, ftill a Secret to the Generality of the World, he was thrown out of all ; and the Prin-

B 3   cefs

† See the Hift. of *Eng.* Vol. III. p. 530.

cefs of *Denmark* (now Queen) in Difgrace with the King, and her Sifter the Queen, for taking his and his Lady's Part.

Towards the End of King *William*'s Reign, he was reftored to his Majefty's Favour, and was made Governour to the Duke of *Gloucefter*, one of the Lords Juftices, and Plenipotentiary in *Holland*.

On the Queen's Acceffion to the Throne, he was made Captain-General of all the Forces, created a Duke, had the Garter, and Mafter of Ordnance.

He is a tall, handfom Man for his Age, with a very obliging Addrefs; of a wonderful Prefence of Mind, fo as hardly ever to be difcompofed; of a very clean Head, and found Judgment; very bold, never daunted for want of Succefs; every Way capable of being a Great Man, if the great Succefs of his Arms, and the Heaps of Favours thrown upon him by

his

his Sovereign, does not raife his Thoughts
above the reft of the Nobility, and confequently draw upon him the Envy of
the People of *England.* He is turned
of Fifty Years of Age.

As *England* owes entirely to his Conduct, the making that great Turn of
Affairs at the *Revolution,* without the
fhedding of Blood ; fo does all *Europe,*
the faving the Empire, by his quick
Reduction of the Bifhop of *Cologne.*
His March to the *Danube,* and reducing
of *Bavaria* was his own Contrivance,
and executed with a Bravery hardly
to be paralleled in any Hiftory, hath
got him fo great Reputation, as to
make him alfo the growing Hopes of
Italy, which growns under the Weight
of the prefent *French* Power.

Detestably Covatous.

James,

James, Duke of *Ormond*, Lord Lieutenant of *Ireland*,

IS Grandſon to that Duke who was Lord-Lieutenant moſt of King *Charles* the Second's Reign, and Son to the Earl of *Oſſory*, who was General in *Holland*.

He was, when very young, choſen by the Univerſity of *Oxford* to be their Chancellor; and, to his Power, then opępoſed the Growth of *Popery*, and the Deſpotic Meaſures of King *James*'s Court, which he left, along with Prince *George*, at the Revolution, and declared for the Laws and Liberties of his Country.

All King *William*'s Reign he was a faithful Follower of his Perſon, and for him; attended him in all his Campaigns; was Captain of his Horſe-Guards, Gen-

tleman

tleman of his Bed Chamber, and Lieutenant-General of his Army. His Ex-
pences were fo great Abroad, that it
may be faid, he gained more Reputation by his Generofity, than many Ge-
nerals have by their Armies; and did
a great deal of Honour to his Country,
to the leffening his own Eftate.

On the Queen's Acceffion to the
Throne, he had the Command given
him of the Expedition to *Cadiz*; which
mifcarried not by his Fault, as appeared
plainly in the Examination of that Affair in the Houfe of Peers; and he had
the good Luck in his Return, to burn
the *French* Fleet at *Vigo*, and to affift at
the folemn *Te Deum*, fung by the *Queen*
at St. *Paul's* for that Expedition; when
it appeared how much he was the Dar-
ling of the People, who neglected their
Sovereign, and applauded him more, perhaps, than ever any Subject was on any
Occafion.

He

the *Revolution*, with the Prince of *Orange*; and although very young, was, to the general Satisfaction of the People, made fole Secretary of State.

The King, fome little Time after his coming to the Crown, fell in with a Set of People that oppofed him, this Gentleman would not mix with them, but threw down the *Seals*; and, after leading a quiet Life for fome Years, was with great Difficulty prevailed on to take them up again; was created a Duke, had the Garter, and Prefident of the Council; till an unhappy Fall from his Horfe, fo bruifed him, as to render him uncapable to attend Bufinefs, for which Reafon he preffed the King to be difcharged from his weighty Office, and was made Lord *Chamberlain* : But his fpitting of Blood continuing to a violent Degree, he was neceffitated to give up all his Employments.

His

His leaving *England* at a Time when he *Partition Treaty* began to be quef-ioned, gave Occafion for his Enemies o fay, that he fled from the Storm ; ınd yet his Intereft was fo great in the *Houfe of Commons*, that his very Name ıad thrown the *Impeachment* out, if the ıdverfe Party had not, for that very Rea-ŏn, kept it out of the *Impeachment* : And King *William* was ufed to fay, That the Duke of *Shrewsbury* was the only Man he *Whigs* and *Tories* both fpoke well of.

The Manner of the *French* King's ːeceiving him at *Verfailles*, gave a Han-dle to his Enemies, to fay, That he was ſtill in fome Intrigue of State : And King *William* obliging him to go to *that* Court, contrary to his Inclination, looked ıs if the King was in the Plot, to ren-der him fufpected to the People : As his going to *Rome* made them fay, he was declared a *Roman Catholic* again.

He

Charles, Duke of *Somerset,* Mafter of the Horfe,

OF the Antient Family of *Seymour,* who made fo great a Figure in the Reign of *Edward* the Sixth.

This Duke, in the Reign of King *Charles* the Second, had the Garter, and married the Heirefs of *Piercy* of *Northumberland,* which much increafed his Eftate, but he made no confiderable Figure, till the Reign of King *James,* when, being in Waiting as Bed-chamberman, at the arrival of the *Pope's Nuncio* in *England,* and refufing to affift at the Ceremony of the Introduction, he was difmiffed from all his Employments.

He notwithftanding did not enter into the Meafures of the *Revolution,* but for fome Years warmly oppofed the De-

Defigns of King *William's* Miniftry; joined in Impeaching the *Partition,* and protefted againft acquitting thofe who advifed it.

Yet, upon the *French* King's fending the Duke of *Anjou* to *Spain,* he came over to the Service of his Country, and was made Prefident of the Council, and joined with a great deal of Zeal, in the Methods concerted for preventing the Growing Power of *France.*

On the Queen's Acceffion to the Throne, he was made Mafter of the Horfe; and appears at Court with a great deal of Warmth, for a Party that feems to fuffer by King *William's* Death.

He is of a middle Stature, well Sha-ped, a very Black Complexion, a lover of Mufick and Poetry; of good Judg-ment, but by Reafon of a great Hefi-tation in his Speech, wants Expreffion. He is about Forty-two Years old.

C   *Wil-*

William, Duke of *Devonſhire*, Lord Steward of the Houſhold,

WAS always a firm Aſſertor of the Liberties of his Country, and the *Proteſtant* Religion, for which he met with ſeveral Hardſhips in King *James*'s Reign. He took up Arms at the *Revolution*, and was by King *William* created Duke, and had the Garter. Was Lord Steward of the Houſhold all that Reign, as he is ſtill to the Queen

He hath been the fineſt and hand-ſomeſt Gentleman of his Time ; loves the Ladies, and Plays ; keeps a noble Houſe, and Equipage ; is tall, well made, and of a princely Behaviour. Of nice Honour in every Thing, but the pay-ing his Tradeſmen. Paſt Sixty Years old.

John

John, Duke of *Buckinghamſhire*, &c. Lord Privy Seal,

W AS Earl of *Mulgrave* in the Reign of King *Charles* the Second, had the Garter, and made a conſiderable Figure at Court. His Preſumption made him make Love to the Princeſs *Anne* (now Queen) for which he left the Kingdom; but ſoon after returned, and was made Lord Chamberlain by King *James*.

He oppoſed the *Revolution*; nor did he ever enter into the Meaſures of the Court all King *William*'s Reign, yet was created by that King, Marquiſs of *Normanby*.

On the Queen's Acceſſion to the Throne, he was made of the Cabinet, Lord Privy Seal, and Duke of *Buckinghamſhire*.

C 2   He

He is a Nobleman of Learning, and good Natural Parts, but of no Principles.   Violent for the *High-Church*, yet feldom goes to it.   Very proud, infolent, and covetous, and takes all Advantages.   In paying his Debts, unwilling; and is neither efteemed nor beloved :   For, notwithftanding his great Intereft at Court, it is certain he hath none in either Houfe of Parliament, or in the Country.   He is of a middle Stature, of a Brown Complexion, with a four, lofty Look.   Near Sixty Years old.

This Character the trueft of any.

Thomas, Earl of _Pembroke_, Prefident of the Council,

IS the Reprefentative of the Ancient Family of the _Herberts_ in _Wales_, being born a younger Brother; he applied himfelf to the Law, and the Knowledge of the Conftitution of his Country; but his Brother's Death brought him into the Houfe of Peers, where he makes a good Figure.

He was made Lord Privy Seal by King _William_, and in fome Time after, Prefident of the Council: Was Firft Plenipotentiary at the Treaty of _Ryfwick_; and, after prefiding fome Years at the Board of Admiralty, our moft able Seamen fay, That he only wanted the Experience of going to Sea, to make the beft Admiral we have.

He

He is a good Judge in all the feveral Sciences ; is a great Encourager of Learning and Learned Men ; a lover of the Conftitution of his Country, without being of a Party, and yet efteemed by all Parties.   His Life and Converfation being after the Manner of the *Primitive Chriftians* ;   Meek in his Behaviour, Plain in his Drefs ; fpeaks little ; of a good Countenance, though very ill Shaped ; tall, thin, and ftoops. About Fifty Years old.

Sidney, Lord *Godolphin*, Lord High Treasurer of *England*,

IS the Second Son of a good Family in *Cornwal*, was Page to King *Charles* the Second; ever of great Application in the Improvement of Knowledge, and understood perfectly every Thing he understood.

When he was but very young, King *Charles* employed him in the Affairs of the Publick, and sent him to *Holland* on a Negotiation, that procured the Trust of .... and during his Reign, and the two other succeeding, he was often employed in the Management of the Revenue, which he still carried unblemished, never had any share in .... or was .... in King *James* .... with King *William* kept .... better .... Nation in ....

This Queen has deſervedly made him Lord High Treaſurer; in which Station he hath ſo improved the Revenue, and put it into ſo good a Method, notwith-ſtanding the Debts of the Nation, that Money is lent to the Publick at Five *per Cent.*

He was made a Baron by King *Charles* the Second, and in all Reigns has refu-ſed any higher Titles, as he did the Garter of the preſent Queen, which he hath ſince accepted of.

He hath an admirable, clear Under-ſtanding, of ſlow Speech, with an awful, ſerious Deportment; does more than he promiſes; an Enemy to Flattery, Shew and Violence; of very hard Acceſs; but that being equally denied to all De-grees of People, makes it ſupportable; of a low Stature; thin, with a very black and ſtern Countenance. Near Sixty Years old.

Dan-

Daniel, Earl of *Nottingham,* Secretary of State,

IS eldest Son to Mr. *Finch,* Lord Chancellor in the Reign of King *Charles* the Second. This Gentleman never made any confiderable Figure, till the *Revolution,* when he zealoufly oppofed King *William's* coming to the Throne, yet was made Secretary of State by that Prince, to oblige the *Church,* of which he fets up for a mighty Champion.

After about three Years ferving in this Poft, the Jealoufies of the People of his being in the *French* Intereft, obliged the King to throw him out again. He oppofed the Abjuration of the Prince of *Wales* to that Degree, that he fhed Tears when the Bill paffed, yet took that Oath on the Queen's Acceffion to the Throne, and was made Secretary of State

State again ; but the Jealoufy of tl
People ftill continuing, and the Hou
of Peers fhewing theirs alfo, in the A
fairs of the *Scots* Plot, he laid down tl
Seals.

He is a zealous Promoter of Abfolu
Power in the *State*, and Implicit Fair
in the *Church*, to that Degree, as hardl
to be in common Charity with thofe (
more moderate Principles.

He hath alfo the exterior Air of Bu
finefs, and Application enough to mak
him very capable. In his Habit an
Manners very formal ; a tall, thin, ver
black Man, like a *Spaniard* or *Jeu*
about Fifty Years old.

He fell in with the Whigs, was an
endlefs Talker

Edward

Edward, Earl of *Jerfey*, late Lord Chamberlain,

IS Son to the late Sir *Edward Villers*, a
Relation of the late Duke of *Buckingham/bire*. He was fome confiderable Time
a Servant in the Prince of *Orange's* Family
in *Holland* ; came over at the *Revolution*; was made Gentleman of the Horfe
to the Princefs *Mary*, then made Queen:
He continued in that Poft till her Death,
and was then made one of the Lords
Juftices; and in fome Time after, was
fent Plenipotentiary to *Holland*, and created Earl of *Jerfey*.

He relieved my Lord *Portland*, in his
Embaffy to *France* ; and at his Return
to *England* was made Secretary of State,
and in fome little Time after, Lord
Chamberlain.

Although

Although he was principally concerned in the making the *Partition Treaty*, yet he was very Active in the Impeaching of Thofe, who, its thought, advifed it, and was the Handle by which the great Turn then made in the Adminiftration was occafioned.

On the Queen's Acceffion to the Throne, he was continued in his Office of Lord Chamberlain ; but doth not feem to have great Intereft at Court, nor is much regarded out of his Office.

He hath gone through all the Great Offices of the Kingdom, with a very ordinary Underftanding ; was employed by one of the greateft Kings that ever was in Affairs of the greateft Confequence, and yet a Man of a weak Capacity. He makes a good Figure in his Perfon, being tall, well fhaped, handfome, and dreffes clean ; and fince the writing of thefe Characters, he is turned out, and fucceeded by the Earl of *Kent*. He is turned of Forty-five Years old. Law-

Lawrence, Earl of *Rochester*,

IS Second Son to Chancellor *Hyde*, Lord *Clarendon*, and Uncle to the prefent Queen; one that hath had all the Improvement of Education and Experience, with a good Capacity. He was, when very young, employed by King *Charles* the Second in Foreign Negotiations; and by King *James* made Lord High Treafurer of *England*, had 'the Garter, and created Earl of *Rochester*.

He oppofed King *William's* coming to the Throne, and generally thwarted the Meafures of that Court, till the King, to gain him and his Party, in Oppofition to *France*, upon the Breach of the *Partition-Treaty*, made him Lord Lieutenant of *Ireland*, and of the Cabinet; but notwithftanding Expectation, he was thrown out again; yet had always a very confiderable Penfion during that King's Reign.   On

On the Queen's Acceffion to
Throne, he was again made Lord Li
tenant of *Ireland*, which he foon qi
ted; and not being made Lord H
Treafurer, which he expected, he wa
difgufted, as not to come more to Coi

He is eafily wound up to a Paffi
which is the Reafon why he often lo
himfelf in the Debates of the Houfe
Peers ; and the oppofite Party knew
well how to attack him, as to make
great Stock of Knowledge fail him.
is, notwithftanding, one of the fii
Men in *England* for Intereft, efpeci
the *Church-Party*, and is very zealous
his Friends. He is of a middle Stati
well Shaped, of a Brown Complexi
and about Sixty Years old.

Thomas, Duke of Leeds,

WAS Sir *Thomas Osborne*, of a good Family in *Yorkshire*, and brought to Court by the late Duke of *Buckinghamshire*, in the Reign of King *Charles* the Second.

He, with the Lords *Shaftesbury* and *Clifford*, were the Advisers, and Carriers on of that scandalous Part of King *Charles*'s Reign, the shutting up the *Exchequer*. He was made Lord Treasurer, Earl of *Danby*, and had the Garter.

He was Impeached in the *House* of *Commons*, by the present Earl of *Montagu*, then Ambassador in *France*, not only for being a Pensioner of *France* himself, but Advising, and Bargaining for a Pension for the King his Master also; and was on this Impeachment sent to the *Tower*, where he lay many Years.

At

At the *Revolution* he declared for
William, was taken into Favour by
Prince, made a Duke, and Prefider
the Council : But the People's S
cions of his being in the *French* Inte
his taking a Bribe of Six Thou
Pounds to pafs the *Eaft-India* Cha
with fome other Reafons, threw
out of all.

He is a Gentleman of admii
Natural Parts, great Knowledge
Experience in the Affairs of his
Country, but of no Reputation with
Party.

Since the Queen's Acceffion to
Throne, he hath not been regarded
though he took his Place at the Coui
Board. He hath been very handfc
and is near Seventy Years old.

Earl of *Romney,*

IS a Third Son of the Earl of *Leicef-ter*'s Family, and Brother to that fa-mous *Algernon Sidney,* who was Be-headed.

In the Reign of King *Charles* the Se-cond, he was efteemed one of the fineft Gentlemen of that Court, and was a great Favourite of the Dutchefs of *York,* Daughter to Chancellor *Hyde.* He was Envoy from the King to the Prince of *Orange*; at whofe Court he made fo good an Intereft, that when the *Popifh* Party began to prevail, and his Family to fuffer in *England,* he returned thi-ther, and was more in Truft and Con-fidence with the Prince, than any *Eng-lifhman.*

He made a Journey to *Italy* a Year before the *Revolution,* for the Prince of *Orange*'s Intereft, and carried on feveral

D   In-

Intrigues, under the Pretence of the *Carnival* of *Venice*, with Princes who were then entering into that Confederacy. He alfo made two or three Journies in Difguife into *England*, and was indeed the great *Wheel* on which the *Revolution* rolled King *William* made him Colonel of his Foot-Guards, Secretary of State, Gentleman of his Bed-chamber, Warden of the *Cinque-Forts* ; fent him once Lord Lieutenant of *Ireland*, and afterwards made him Groom of the Stole, Mafter of the Ordnance, and Lieutenant-General of his Army.

On the Queen's Acceffion to the Throne, he was ftripped of all but the Foot-Guards. He is a Gentleman that hath lived up to the Employments the King gave him ; of great Honour and Honefty, with a moderate Capacity, who promifed every Body, but did for no one which makes him the lefs pitied ; conftantly, for many Years, drunk once a
Day ;

Day; a tall handfome Man for his Age, being turned of Sixty Years old.

Since the writing of thefe Characters, this Gentleman died, and is fucceeded in the Guards by the Prince of *Denmark*.

John, Duke of *Newcaftle*,

IS of the Name of *Holles*, was Earl of *Clare* before the *Revolution* ; and married a Daughter of the late Duke of *Newcaftle*'s, who died without Heirs Male. King *William* created this Gentleman a Duke, and gave him the Garter.

He hath the beft Eftate in *England*, and employs moft of his Time in improving it ; is very covetous, yet makes a great Figure at his Seat in *Yorkfhire* ; is firm for the Conftitution of his Country ; and hath one only Daughter, who will be the richeft Heirefs in *Europe*. He is a black, ruddy complexioned Man, near Sixty Years old.

D 2

Charles,

Charles Lenos, Duke of *Richmond*.

IS Son to King *Charles* the Second, by the Dutchefs of *Portfmouth*; he was carried by his Mother into *France*, in the Reign of King *James*, and left *France* in the Reign of King *William*, when he declared himfelf for the Religion and Conftitution of his Country.

He is a Gentleman Good-natured to a Fault; very well bred, and hath many valuable Things in him; is an Enemy to Bufinefs, very credulous, well Shaped, Black Complexion, much like King *Charles*; not Thirty Years old.

A Shallow Coxcomb.

Wri-

Wriothefley, Duke of *Bedford,*

IS Son to the Lord *Ruffel* who was Beheaded in the Reign of King *Charles* the Second, and Grandfon to the late Duke of *Bedford.* The Queen made him Lord High Conftable, and gave him the Garter.

He loves Play, and doth not feem to have any Inclination for Bufinefs. He gave his Vote in the Bill againft *Occafional Conformity,* although the Party he Voted with, took off his Father's Head. He hath feen the World, and hath made good Reflections when he pleafes to make Ufe of them. He has one of the greateft Eftates in *England* ; is of low Stature, fair Complexion, not Thirty Years old.

Charles,

Charles, Duke of Bolton,

IS the Reprefentative of *Powlet,*
good Family in *England.*   He e͞n
tred early into the Meafures for favi͞n
his Country in King *James*'s Reig͟n
and, at the *Revolution,* was made Lo͞r
Chamberlain to King *William*'s Quee͞n
in which Poft he continued   duri͞n
her Life ; was afterwards fent one o
the Lords Juftices to *Ireland,* but do͞e
not now make any Figure at Court,
nor any where else, is a great Booby.
He is very warm for the Conftitu͞n
tion of his Country ; is of a free an͞d
familiar Difpofition ; of low Stature
fair Complexion, about Forty Yea͞r
old.

George *Fitzroy*, Duke of *Northumberland*,

IS Son to King *Charles* the Second, by the Dutchefs of *Cleveland* ; was one of the Captain's of King *James's* Horfe-Guards, which he quitted at the Revolution, and never had any Poft, though fometimes Prefents from the King, all King *William's* Reign.

On the Queen's Acceffion to the Throne, he was made Conftable of *Windfor-Caftle*, and Lieutenant-General ; and had my Lord of *Oxford's* Regiment of Horfe.

He is a Man of Honour, nice in paying his Debts, and living well with his Neighbours in the Country ; does not much care for the Converfation of Men of Quality, or Bufinefs. Is a tall Black Man, like his Father the King, about Forty Years old.

D

He was a moft worthy Perſon, very good with h had cood Senſe.

Charles, Duke of St. *Albans,*

IS Son to King *Charles* the Second, by
Mrs. *Gwyn* ; was made by King
William one of the Bed-chamber, and Captain of the *Band* of *Penſioners;* and ſent
by that King to *France,* to congratulate
the Marriage of the Duke of *Burgundy.*

He is a Gentleman every Way *de bon
Naturel,* well-bred, doth not love Buſi-
neſs ; is well-affected to the Conſtitu-
tion of his Country. He is of a Black
Complexion, not ſo tall as the Duke of
Northumberland, yet very like King *Charles.*
Turned of Thirty Years old.

Charles Fitzroy, Duke of *Grafton,*

IS Grandſon to King *Charles* the Second,
and Son to the Heirs of *Bennet,* Earl
of *Arlington :* Is a very pretty Gentleman, hath been Abroad in the World ;
zealous for the Conſtitution of his Country. A tall Black Man, about Twenty-
five Years old. Sir

*Almoſt a Slobberer without one good
Quality.*

Sir *Nathan Wright*, Lord-Keeper,

IS Son of a *Clergyman*, a good common Lawyer, a flow Chancellor, and no Civilian. Chance more than Choice brought him the Seals: The Lords Chief Justices *Holt* and *Treby* refusing to succeed so Great a Man as the Lord *Somers*, they fell into the Hands of this Gentleman, who being recommended by the opposite Party, proved their faithful Tool ever since.

He is a plain Man, both in Person and Conversation, of middle Stature, inclining to Fat, hath a fat broad Face, much marked with the Small-pox.

– very covetous.

He

He hath done a great deal of Goo
to his private Family fince he w
Keeper, having married his Son an
Daughter to very confiderable Fortune
got the Employment of *Clerk of the Crou*
in Parliament for his Son, and beftow
the beft Livings in the Queen's Gift c
his poor Relations.

Joh

John, Duke of *Montagu*,

IS the Reprefentative of the Family
of *Montagu* in *England*, made a confiderable Figure in the Houfe of *Commons*, and at Court in King *Charles*
the Second's Reign, and was Ambaffador twice from that King to the Court
of *France* ; but that Party growing too
hard for him, obliged him to fly his
Country in that Reign, and he continued *incognito* all That, and King *James's*.
After the *Revolution* he was created
from a Baron to be Earl of *Montagu*,
and reftored to his Place of Mafter of
the *Wardrobe*, which he bought in the
Reign of King *Charles* for Life, and was
fufpended by King *James* ; is of the
Privy-Council.

He is a great Supporter of the *French*,
and other *Proteftants* who are drove into *England*, by the Tyranny of their
Princes ;

Princes ; an Admirer of Learning, a
Learned Men, efpecially the *Beaux Efpri*
and the *Belles Lettres.* A good Juc
of *Architecture* and, *Painting*, as his fi
Pictures at his Houfes in *Northamptc*
fhire and *London* do fhow. He hath o
of the beft Eftates in *England*, which
knows very well how to improve.
of a middle Stature, inclining to F
of a courfe, dark Complexion.

Since this Queen's Acceffion to t
Throne, he hath been created a Dul
and is near Sixty Years old.

As amant as I have as any his time.

Meinha

Meinhardt Sconbergh, Duke of Sconbergh and *Linſter*,

IS of a good *German* Family, and born in *France* ; Son to that *Sconbergh* who was Mareſchal of *France*, afterwards Stadtholder of *Pruſſia* ; who came over at the *Revolution* with King *William,* and was killed at the Battle of the *Boyne* in *Ireland*.

This Gentleman was created Duke of *Linſter*, by King *William* ; and after his Brother's Death, who was killed in *Savoy,* was a Peer in *England* by the Title of Duke *Sconbergh*.

He never was in Action all King *William*'s Reign, but left by that Prince his General of all the Forces in *England*, when his Majeſty went Abroad.

When

John, Lord *Somers*, late Lord Chancellor,

OF a creditable Family, in the City of *Worcester*; his Father was an Attorney, and bred him to the Law which was his Profeſſion for ſome Years before he was taken notice of He wa retained as one of the Counſel for the ſeven Biſhops in King *James*'s Reign and behaved himſelf, in that Cauſe, with ſo much Applauſe, as gained him a very great Reputation, and firſt brought him into Buſineſs.

On King *William*'s Acceſſion to the Throne, he was made Attorney General Lord Keeper, Lord Chancellor, and a Peer; and was for many Years Chie in the Adminiſtration of publick Af fairs.

H

He gained fuch a Reputation of Honefty with the Majority of the People of
England, that it may be faid, very few
Minifters in any Reign ever had fo
many Friends in the Houfe of Commons ; or could go to the City, and, on
their bare Word, gain fo much Credit
of the Publick. He is believed to be the
beft Chancellor that ever fat in the Chair,
and as knowing in the Affairs of foreign
Courts, as in the Laws of his own
Country. He gave Entertainments to
foreign Minifters, more like one always bred up in a Court, than at a
Bar; and ufed often to treat People
at his Table, of feveral Profeffions, as
if it were the only Thing he ever had
ftudied. Such a Force of Expreffion,
that he convinces at the fame Time he
informs; and all his Arguments fo re-
gular, that like Geometrical Stairs, they
fupport one another; yet this Gentleman (as all *Englifh* Chief Minifters generally are) was envied, and often ftruck

E   againft

againſt by the Houſe of Commons, the Affair of *Kidd* *, and the Partition, with the paſſing of Grants in his own Favour, were the great Weapons made uſe of againſt him, but he had warded the Blow, if the King, by his taking the Seals from him, had not ſeemed to have approved of the Proceeding.

Being diſcharged from all his Employments, he ſtill keeps up a great Intereſt in both Houſes. A Thing very uncommon for an *Engliſh* diſgraced Miniſter.

He is of a grave Deportment, eaſy, and free in Converſation; ſomething of a Libertine, of middle Stature, brown Complexion, near fifty Years old.

---

* The Proceedings againſt Captain *Kidd*, the noted Pirate.

I allow him to have poſſeſs'd all Excellent Qualifications except Virtue, He had Violent paſſions, & hardly Subdued them by his great Prudence.

Charles

Charles, Lord *Halifax,*

IS a younger Son to a very honourable Family in *Northamptonſhire,* and Grandſon to an Earl of *Mancheſter,* he had his Education at the Univerſity of *Cambridge,* where, writing a Satire, called, *The City Mouſe and Country Mouſe,* in Anſwer to *Dryden's Hind and Panther,* in King *James's* Reign, he was much taken notice of, and, at the Revolution, brought to Court. His natural Quickneſs, Eloquence, and good Addreſs, gained him the King's Favour; and being choſen a Member of Parliament, he ſoon began to make a conſiderable Figure in the Houſe of Commons.

His Majeſty made him Commiſſioner of the Treaſury. It is to him the King owes the great Loans that were made to the Crown, the eſtabliſhing the Paper

E. 2   Credit,

Credit, and the Debentures; as the Na
tion doth the recoining our Money, a
the Time they were engaged in so ex
penfive a War, all of them fuch mafterl
Strokes, and ferves anfwering the End
for which they were defigned, that the
fhew him a wonderful Man, of fuch
powerful Eloquence, that he could turi
the Houfe of Commons which Way h
pleafed, and almoft never miffed th
Point he aimed at.

But as all Courtiers, who rife to
quick, as he did, are envied, fo hi
great Favour with the King, and powei
ful Intereft in the Houfe, raifed a grea
Party againft him, which he ftrengthen
ed, by feeming to defpife them.

The Deficiency of Parliamentai
Funds, and the growing Debts of th
Nation, by the great Intereft of Pap
Credit, laid him but too much open t
their Attacks, he having the whole A
miniftration of the Revenue.

Whe

When he faw the Party growing too
ftrong for him in the Houfe of Commons, he prudently got himfelf made
a Lord; and as a Screen from all Ob-
jections againft his Adminiftration,
quitted his Management of Commiflio-
ner, to ferve as Auditor: But his Enemies did not quit him fo, they followed him into the Houfe of Peers with an
Impeachment, and left no Stone un-
turned, to get him out of his Employ,
befpattering him every Day with Pam-
phlets.

He is a Gentleman of great natural
Parts, Learning and Dexterity in Bufinefs; one of the fitteft Minifters in the
World to help a Prince through a War,
having a very projecting Head. His
quick Rife made him haughty, and by
fome thought violent; and what helped
to pull him down, he could not endure
an Equal in Bufinefs: My Lord <i>Sun-
derland</i> helped to eftablifh him with the
King, and he endeavouring afterwards
to

to throw his Lordſhip out of the Adminiſtration, made that Lord join to trip
'up his Heels.

He is a great Encourager of Learning
and learned Men, is the Patron of the
Muſes, of very agreeable Converſation,
a ſhort fair Man, not forty Years old.

encouragements were only good words
without. I never heard him ſay one
thing, or ſeen to taſte what was
d by another.

Charles

Charles, Earl of *Dorfet* and *Middlefex,*

WAS efteemed one of the fineft Gentlemen, in *England,* in the Reign of King *Charles* the Second; of great Learning, extremely witty, and *Small hous* hath been the Author of fome of the fineft Poems in the *Englifh* Language; efpecially *Satire.* The *Mecænas,* and Prince of our *Englifh* Poets, and as Lord *Rochefter* faid of him very juftly, was, *The* beft *good Man, with the* worft *natur'd Mufe.*

He hardly appeared in the Reign of King *James.* King *William* gave him the Garter, made him Lord Chamberlain, often of the Cabinet, and one of the Lords Juftices in his Abfence. Some Years before the King's Death he retired from Bufinefs, nor does he come to Court in the Reign of this Queen He is ftill one of the pleafanteft Companions in the World, when he likes his Company. He is very fat, troubled with the Spleen, and turned of fixty Years old.

Not of late Years but a very dull one.

Charles,

Charles, Earl of *Manchester*,

IS defcended from one of the firft Families (of the Name of *Montagu*)had Command of the Yeomen of Guards en him at the Revolution; was fent ambaffador Extraordinary to *Venice*, fucceded my Lord *Jerfey* in his Embaffy to *France*, and was made Secretary of State.

On the Queen's Acceffion to the throne, he was difcharged of all his employments.

He is a Gentleman of greater Application than Capacity ; of good Addrefs, but no Elocution; is very honeft, a Lover of the Conftitution of his Country, which he takes Pains to underftand and ferve; is of middle Stature, well fhaped, with a very beautiful Countenance, fair Complexion, about forty years old.

Francis

Francis Newport, Earl of *Bradford*,

WAS created Lord *Newport* by King *Charles* the Second, and one of the fineſt Gentlemen of that Court; was neglected in the Reign of King *James*; but at the Revolution made Lord Treaſurer of the Houſhold, and Cofferer, and created Earl of *Bradford*.

He hath a great deal of Wit, is a juſt Critic, a Judge and Lover of Poetry, Painting, and nice Living; hath been a handſome Man, but is now near eighty Years old, was always a great Libertine.

Charles

Charles Howard, Earl of *Carliſle,*

IS a Branch of the noble Family of the *Howards* (Dukes of *Norfolk*) was one of the Gentlemen of the Bed-Chamber to King *William*; and under that Pretence, went over to *Holland,* the laſt Year of the King's Life, and ſollicited the Diſſolution of that Parliament, which impeached the *Partition Treaty,* and obtained it of the King. He was the great Inſtrument of procuring, from the Country, the *Addreſſes,* upon the *French* King's declaring the Prince of *Wales,* and was made firſt Commiſſioner of the Treaſury.

On the Queen's Acceſſion to the Throne, he was diſmiſſed from his Employments at Court. He is a Gentleman of Great Intereſt in the Country, and very Zealous for its Welfare, hath a fine Eſtate, and a very good Underſtanding, with a grave Deportment; is of a middle Stature, fair Complexion, turned of fifty Years old.

Richard Savage, Earl *Rivers,*

HIS Father being alive in King *James*'s Reign, he was Lord *Colchester,* and a Colonel of Horse, and was the first who joined King *William* at the *Revolution;* was made one of the Captains of the Horse Guards, attended the King all his Campaigns, and was Lieutenant General of the Army. On the Queen's Accession to the Throne, he was continued in all his Employments, but after serving one Campaign, he laid them all down.

He was one of the greatest Rakes in *England* in his younger Days, but always a Lover of the Constitution of his Country; is a Gentleman of very good Sense, and very cunning; brave in his Person, a Lover of Play, and understands it perfectly well; hath a very good Estate, and improves it every Day; something covetous; is a tall handsome Man, and of a very fair Complexion. He is turned of forty Years old.

a rank Knave in Common dealing, & William & Prostitute.

William, Earl of *Portland*,

IS a Gentleman of the Name of *Ben-tinck* in *Holland*, was Page to King *William*, when Prince of *Orange*; and by his affiduous Fidelity came to be his chief Favourite. His Majefty made him a Peer of *England*, and gave him the Garter, threw away fuch Grants of Lands on him, as obliged the Parliament to interpofe, and put a Stop to them.

He gave him the abfolute and intire Government of *Scotland*, made him a Lieutenant General, firft Lord of his Bed-Chamber, and Privy Purfe.

He was fent Ambaffador to *France* againft his Will, being fenfible of the growing Favour of my Lord *Albemarle*, (another *Dutchman* his Enemy) and he
had

had Reafon, for that Lord prevailed fo far in his Abfence, as to oblige him, by feveral little Affronts, to lay down all his Employments: And altho' the King ftill efteemed him, yet it cannot be faid he was any more in Favour all the King's Life.

On the Queen's Acceffion to the Throne, he was turned out of the Poft of Keeper of *Windfor* great Park. He is fuppofed to be the richeft Subject in *Europe*, very profufe in Gardening, Birds, and Houfhold Furniture, but mighty frugal and parfimonious in every Thing elfe; of a very lofty Mien, and yet not proud; of no deep Underftanding, confidering his Experience; neither much beloved nor hated by any Sort of People, *Englifh* or *Dutch*. He is turned of fifty Years old.

A great a Dunce as ever I knew

James

James Stanley Earl of *Derby*,

WAS Colonel *Stanley*, and Groom of the Bed-Chamber to King *William* all his Reign.

On his Brother's Death he came to the House of Peers, where he never will make any great Figure, the Sword being more his Profession; he is a fair Complexioned Man, well shaped, taller than the ordinary Size, and a Man of Honour.

He is turned of forty Years old

As small a Scoundrel as his Brother.

Charles,

Charles, Earl of *Peterborow*,

WAS Lord *Mordaunt* in the Reign of King *Charles* the Second; then a Lover of the Conftitution of his Country, and a great Projector for the Improvement of our Plantations.

He was very zealous at the *Revolution*, for which King *William* made him Earl of *Monmouth*, and employed him in Places of Truft, till his natural Giddinefs, in running from Party to Party, threw him out.

His promifing Sir *John Fenwick* his Life, if he would accufe the Duke of *Shrewsberry*, and the Lord *Orford*, to have a Defign to bring in King *James* ; and his writing a Book, by the Affiftance of Dr. *D'Avenant*, and putting one *Smith's* Name

Name to it, * againft that Duke, loft him with all honeft Men ; the Houfe of Commons having voted the *one* a fcandalous Defign to make a Difference between the King and his beft Friends, and the Houfe of Peers having ordered the *fecond* to be burnt by the Hands of the common Hangman.

On the Queen's Acceffion to the Throne, my Lord *Nottingham* procured him a Commiffion to be Captain Gene-ral of the Plantations in *America,* and Governour of *Jamaica;* but my Lord *Marlborough* returning from *Holland,* be-fore the Commiffion paffed the Seals, it was ftopped; as being too great a Command for one of his fiery, incon-ftant Temper : This foured him fo, that he oppofeth *this* Court, as he did the *laft.* However, the next Year he ob-tained a Commiffion to command the

F   Defcent,

* It was intitled, *Memoirs of Secret Service.* By *Matthew Smith* of the *Inner Temple,* Efq; 8vo, 1699.

Defcent, for which we attend the Succefs.

He affects Popularity, and loves to
preach in *Coffee-Houfes*, and publick
Places ; is an open Enemy to *Revealed
Religion* ; brave in his Perfon; hath a
good Eftate ; does not feem Expenfive,
yet always in Debt, and very poor. A
well fhaped thin Man, with a very brisk
Look, near Fifty Years old.

Character for the most part

Arnold

Arnold Jooft van Keppel, Earl of *Albemarle.*

IS a Gentleman of the Name of *Keppel,* a good Family in *Guelderland* He came over Page to King *William* at the *Revolution* ; was firft employed in copying Letters, and other fmall Services ; but being fupported by my Lord *Sunderland,* and Mrs. *Villiers,* to pull down my Lord *Portland,* came to be chief Favourite to that Prince, was created a Peer of *England,* and Mafter of the Robes; had the Garter, made General of the *Swiffers* in *Holland,* and had the *Horfe-Guards.*

On the Queen's Acceffion to the Throne, he was continued in his Command of the Guards, and affifted as firft Captain at her Coronation, and continues General of the *Swifs* in *Holland.* He was King *William*'s conftant Companion in all his Diverfions and Plea-

F 2   fures;

my Infamous Pleasures.

fures; and intrufted, at laft, with Affairs of the greateft Confequence; had a great Influence over the King; is beautiful in his Perfon; open and free in his Converfation; very expenfive in his Manner of Living; about Thirty Years old.

Charles

Charles Spencer, Earl of *Sunderland*.

[S Son to that great Earl who made fo confiderable a Figure in *England*, n all the Three Reigns of King *Charles*, King *James*, and King *William*, who lied at the Beginning of Queen *Anne's* Reign.

This Gentleman is endued with a great deal of Learning, Virtue, and *720* good Senfe ; very honeft, and zealous for the Liberty of the People ; made a good Figure in the Houfe of Commons, when Lord *Spencer*, and does the fame now in the Houfe of Peers : Being one the Nation repofes great Confidence in ; fit to be a Minifter of State; very fair Complexioned ; middle Stature ; married a Daughter of the Duke of *Marlborough*. He is turned of Thirty Years old.

Alger-

Algernon Capell, Earl of *Essex.*

his Throat IS Son to that Earl whose Throat was cut in the *Tower* in the Reign of King *Charles* the Second. This Gentleman was one of the Bed-chamber to King *William* all his Reign; attended him all his Campaigns, and had a Regiment of Dragoons. He is a good Companion; loves the Interest of his Country; hath no Genius for Business, nor will ever apply himself that Way. He married my Lord *Portland*'s Daughter.

The Queen continues him in his Regiment, and has made him Brigadier-General. He is a well-bred Gentleman, brown Complexioned, and well shaped; but his Mouth is always open. He is about Thirty Years old.

Baſil Fielding, Earl of *Denbigh.*

IS Repreſentative of the Name and Family of *Fielding.* He was Gen-leman of the Horſe to the Prince in the Reign of King *William* ; but on the Dif-ference between the King and him, quitted that Family, and hath a Regiment of Dragoons; he is a Gentleman of good Nature, but is one of the great-eſt Drinkers in *England* ; he is tall, fat, very black, and turned of forty Years old.

Edward Hyde, Earl of *Clarendon,*

IS eldeſt Son to the late Chancellor *Hyde,* and Uncle to the Queen; he was a Nonjuror all King *William*'s Reign, as he is in This. Was Lord Lieutenant of *Ireland* in the Reign of King *Charles* the Second, hath Wit, but Affectation. He is near ſeventy Years old.

F 4   *Thomas*

Thomas Grey, Earl of *Stamford.*

IS one of the firſt Branchesof the *Greys,* a noble Family in *England.* This Gentleman was a Priſoner in the Tower in the Reign of King *Charles* the Second, by the prevalency of the Popiſh Party, anc continued in Diſgrace from the Cour all the Reign of King *James;* he wa very active for the *Revolution,* and wa made by King *William* Chancellor c the Dutchy of *Lancaſter;* his Zeal fo the Publick led him from the Care c his own private Affairs, which he di not mend by his Employment. O the Queen's Acceſſion to the Thron he was diſmiſſed from his Employment.

He doth not want Senſe; but by Rea ſon of a Defect in his Speech, wan Elocution; is a very honeſt Man hin ſelf, but very ſuſpicious of every Bod that is not of his Party, for which h is very zealous, jealous of the Power of the Clergy, who, he is afraid, may fome Time or other influence our Civil Government; from a good Eftate he is become very poor, and much in Debt, is fomething above the middle Stature. He is turned of fifty Years old.

He look'd & talk'd like a very weak man, but it was faid he fpoke well at Council.

Richard

Richard Lumley, Earl of *Scarborough*.

OF the Antient and Noble Family of *Lumley*; he was bred up in the Religion of his Family, which had been always *Roman Catholick*, and turned *Proteſtant* at the Time of the Popiſh Plot, in the Reign of King *Charles* the Second.

At the *Revolution*, King *William* created him Earl of *Scarborough*, made him Captain of one of the Troops of Horſe Guards, and Lieutenant General, and one of the Gentlemen of the Bed-chamber: All which Employments he ſold or quitted before Queen *Mary* died, nor hath entered into any in the Reign of this Queen.

He is a Gentleman of very good Senſe, a great Lover of the Conſtitution of his Country, and an Improver of Trade,

Trade, and his Genius lay very much this Way; a handsome Man, of a brown Complexion, turned of fifty Years old.

Earl of *Kingston.*

OF the Name and Family of *Pierpoint*, hath a very good Eſtate, is a very fine Gentleman, of good Senſe, well bred, and a Lover of the Ladies; intirely in the Intereſt of his Country, makes a good Figure, is of a black Complexion, well made, not forty Years old.

Edward,

Edward, Earl of *Orford*.

IS a Brother's Son of the late Duke of *Bedford*, and bred up to Sea; he was Captain of a Ship in the Reign of King *Charles* the Second, and a Groom of the Bed-Chamber to the Duke of *York*; but upon my Lord *Ruſſel's* being beheaded 1683, he left firſt the Duke of *York's* Family, and at the *Revolution* came over with King *William*.

He commanded the Fleet when th *French* were burnt at *La Hogue*, 1692; as alſo the Grand Fleet that wintered at *Cadiz* in *Spain*, was made a Peer by the Title of Earl of *Orford*, and often of the Cabinet, and one of the Juſtices in the King's Abſence.

No Gentleman was ever better beloved by the *Engliſh* Sailors than he, when he had the firſt Command of the Fleet; but he ſoon loſt all by his Pride, and Covetouſneſs; he was a good Patron to thoſe who depended

imme-

immediately upon him, and loves to be flattered, but irreconcileable to thofe whom he fufpects to be in any other Intereft; this created him a great many Enemies in the Parliament, as well as in the Navy; they called him to Account for the Adminiftration of the Navy in the Mediterranean, and the King faved him by a Privy Seal; he was alfo one of the four Lords impeached for the *Partition*, and thrown out of all his Employments.

Since the Queen's Acceffion to the Throne, he hath been little taken notice of, nor is he pitied by People of his own Profeffion; he hath purchafed a vaft Eftate, and knows very well how to improve it.

He hath a very good Underftanding, but is very paffionate; of a fanguine Complexion, inclining to fat, of a middle Stature, was always in the Intereft of the People by his Votes in both Houfes. He is near fifty Years old.

Arthur,

Arthur, Earl of *Torrington.*

IS a Branch of the Family of *Herbert*, came over Admiral of the Fleet with King *William*, was in Favour, made an Earl, commanded at the *Beachy-Head* Engagement, where we were beat, and he was difgraced for his Conduct therein; and hath never come into Play fince. He is a very fat Man, above fifty Yeas old.

John, Earl of *Leicefter.*

IS the Reprefentative of the Noble Family of *Sidney*. This Gentleman has not been yet in Bufinefs, but behaved himfelf very well, in the Houfe of Commons, when he was Knight of the Shire of *Kent*, his Grandfather and Father being then alive: Is very warm for the Conftitution of his Country, of good Senfe, is of a fair Complexion, and towards thirty-five Years old.

Theophilus,

Theophilus, Earl of *Huntingdon*.

IS the Reprefentative of the Antient Family of *Haftings*; his Father was Captain of the Band of Penfioners to King *James*, and adhered to that Prince's Interelt, after the *Revolution*; for which Reafon this Gentleman his Son left him, and came over to King *William*, who gave him a Company in the Guards, and afterwards a Regiment. He had a Company the firft Year of this Queen's Reign, then threw up his Commiffion; hath a great deal of Wit, with a good Stock of Learning; fpeaks moft of the modern Languages well, underftands the antient, a great Lover of the Liberty of his Country, and is very capable of ferving it when he pleafes to apply himfelf to Bufinefs; of good Addrefs, of a flow lifping Speech, a thin, fmall, fair Complexion, not twenty-five Years old, and fomething of a Libertine.

Thomas

Thomas Tufton, Earl of *Thanet*.

OF the Name of *Tufton*, was born a fourth or fifth Brother, and was in Years before he came to the Honour or Estate. He improves his Estate greatly, which is very considerable; he is a good Country Gentleman, a great Assertor of the Prerogatives of the Monarchy and the Church, a thin, tall, black, red-faced Man, turned of sixty Years old.

of great Piety & Charity.

Edward Montague, Earl of *Sandwich*,

IS a Branch of the Family of *Montague*, and Grandson of that Earl, who was burnt at Sea in the *Soldbay* Engagement 1665. He was Gentleman of Horse to the Prince, of very ordinary Parts, married the witty Lord *Rochester*'s Daughter, who makes him very expensive; a tall, thin, black Man, about thirty-five Years old.

As much a Puppy as ever; Sais, Nicolas very Ugly & a Fop.

Nicholas Leake, Earl of *Scarsdale*,

WAS Gentleman of the Horse to the Princess *Anne* of *Denmark*, (now Queen) at the Revolution, and upon the Prince of *Orange*'s being declared King, threw up all, nor even came into the Measures of the Court, during that Reign.

He was always a Man of Pleasure more than Business, no Man loves the Company of Ladies more than he, or says less when he is in it, yet is successful in his Intrigues; a great Sportsman, and hath neither Genius nor Taste for any Thing else; is of a middle Stature, of a sanguine Complexion, very fat, and forty-five Years old.

Henry Howard, Earl of *Suffolk*,

IS One of the first Branches of the Name of *Howard*, a Gentleman who was never yet in Business, loves Cocking, Horse Matches, and other Country Sports

G, *Richards*

Richard, Earl of *Ranelagh*,

IS a Peer of the Kingdom of *Ireland*, of a great deal of Wit, had originally no great Estate, yet hath spent more Money, built more fine Houses, and laid out more on Houshold-Furniture and Gardening, than any other Nobleman in *England*; he is a great Epicure, and prodigious Expensive; was Paymaster General all the last War, and is above a hundred thousand Pound Sterling in Arrear, which several Parliaments have been calling him to an Account for, yet he escapes with the Punishment only of losing his Place, which the Queen took from him, and divided between Mr. *Fox* and Mr. *Howe.*

He is a bold Man, and very happy in Jests and Repartees, and hath often turned the Humour of the House of Commons, when they have designed to have been very severe. He is very fat, black, and turned of sixty Years old.

Charles,

Charles, Lord *Lucas*,

¯S grand Nephew to Sir *Charles Lucas* who was fhot at *Colchefter*, the Orinal of the Family. This Gentleman is born in *Ireland*, and happened to mmand a Regiment in the *Tower* at e *Revolution*, when an Order came it, that the firft commanding Proteftant fficer in all the Garrifons in *England*, ould take the Command upon him, d all thofe of higher Rank in the wer being Papifts, this Gentleman d the Government during the Time of onfufion, which he managed with fo uch Care and Refpect towards the itizens of *London*, that the Body of the ity recommended him to the King for e Commiffion of Governour, which s Majefty conferred upon him; the raer, that my Lord's Brother dying about is Time, he fucceeded alfo to the erage.

G 2   It

It was great Chance that made him a Lord and Governour of the moſt conſiderable Garriſon in the Nation, both at the ſame Time; to neither of which he could ever have aſpired, if they had not dropt upon him whether he would or not; he made his Court very aſſiduouſly to the King, and by that means he got his Majeſty to excuſe ſeveral Slips which happened in his Government.

He is every way a very plain Man, yet took a great deal of Pains to ſeem knowing and wiſe; every Body pitied him when the Queen turned him out, for his ſeeming good Nature, and real Poverty; he is very fat, very expenſive, and very poor, turned of fifty Years old.

A good plain Humdrum.

Charle

Charles Finch, Earl of *Winchelsea*,

IS of the Family of *Finch*, was brought into the Government by my Lord *Nottingham*, on the Queen's Acceffion to the Throne; when, he was made Warden of the *Cinque-Ports*, under the Prince of *Denmark*, Governour of *Dover* Caftle, and fent Envoy Extraordinary to the Court of *Hanover*.

He hath neither Genius nor Gufto for Bufinefs, loves Hunting and a Bottle, was an Oppofer (to his Power) of the Meafures of King *William*'s Reign, and is zealous for the Monarchy and Church to the higheft Degree.

He loves Jefts and Puns, and that *I nev.* fort of low Wit, is of fhort Stature, well *obferv* fhaped, with a very handfom Counte- *it .* nance, not thirty Years old.

Being very Poor He complied too much with the Party He hated. George

G 3

George Compton, Earl of *Northampton*,

IS Nephew to the Bifhop of *London*, * and a very honeſt Gentleman. He will never make any great Figure, but in his own Houſe, where he entertains his Friends very well. He is a tall, luſty Man, towards forty Years old.

* *Henry Compton*, D.D. Biſhop of *London*, a very worthy Prelate.

George,

George, Lord *Granville*, Lieutenant General of the Ordnance.

I S fecond Son to the Earl of *Bath*, his Education being at Sea. At the *Revolution* he was a Captain of a Ship, ınd made Governour of *Deal-Caftle*, ›ut being chofen a Member of Parliaı nent, and not preferred at Court, as ıe thought he deferved, he turned an ›pen Enemy to the Defigns of King *Wil- iam*; and, by his daring, got himfelf a ĸeputation with that Party; was made ⁊hairman to feveral Committees, and ›nce ftood fair for Speaker.

He was one of Sir *John Fenwick's* ¦reat Advocates againſt the Bill of Atıinder, and one of the Impeachers of thofe ⁊ho advifed the *Partition*, and Manager ·f the Bill for *Occafional Conformity*.

On the Queen's Acceffion to the ⁊hrone, he was made a Privy Counfel-
G 4   lor,

lor, and Lieutenant General of the Artillery, and created a Peer.

He is a Gentleman of tolerable good Senfe, with an undaunted Affurance; very hot for his Party, and Partial; jolly, and of a fair Complexion, middle Stature, inclining to Fat, turned of forty Years old.

Lord *Poulet* of *Hinton*,

WAS made a Privy Counfellor by this Queen, on her Acceffion to the Throne, and is certainly one of the hopefulleft Gentlemen in *England;* is very learned, virtuous, and a Man of Honour; much efteemed in the Country, for his generous way of living with the Gentry, and his Charity to the pooreft fort. He makes but a mean Figure in his Perfon, is of a middle Stature, fair Complexion, not handfome, nor thirty Years old.

This Character is fair enough.   Charles,

Charles, Lord *Townſhend,*

IS a Gentleman of great Learning, attended with a ſweet Diſpoſition; a Lover of the Conſtitution of his Country; is beloved by every Body that knows him, and when once employed in the Adminiſtration of publick Affairs, may ſhew himſelf a great Man. He is tall and handſome, about thirty Years old *.

* His Lordſhip's *Conduct* has fully confirmed the Character here given of Him.

William Legg, Lord *Dartmouth,*

IS Son to that Lord *Dartmouth* who commanded the Fleet in the Reign of King *James* II. On the Queen's Acceſſion to the Throne, was made one of the Lords Commiſſioners of Trade.

He ſets up for a Critick in Converſation, makes Jeſts, and loves to laugh at them; takes a great deal of Pains in his Office, and is in a fair way of riſing at Court; is a ſhort thick Man, of a fair Complexion, turned of thirty-four Years old.

This is right enough but He has little Sincerity.

Heneage Finch, Lord *Guernsey*,

IS second Son of my Lord Chancellor *Finch*, Brother to the Earl of *Nottingham*, and was Sollicitor to King *James* II. He was always a great Opposer of the Measures of King *William*'s Reign, and on the Queen's Accession to the Throne, was made a Peer, by the Title of Lord *Guernsey*.

He is accounted one of the greatest Orators in *England*, and a good common Lawyer; a firm Assertor of the Prerogative of the Crown, and Jurisdiction of the Church; a tall, thin, black Man, splenatick, near fifty Years old.

Thomas

Thomas, Lord *Wharton.*

WAS one of the boldeſt Men in *England* againſt the Meaſures of King *James,* in that Reign; and joined with Zeal at the *Revolution.* He was always at the Head of a great Party in the Houſe of Commons, till by his Father's Death, he was removed to the Houſe of Peers, was Comptroller of the Houſhold all King *William*'s Reign, and very capable of Employments of greater Conſequence and Truſt, being often named to them, but the King as often refuſed it, thinking him too popular, or too much a Republican to be intruſted with the Adminiſtration of State Affairs. Very few Perſons took the Freedom with ſo much Boldneſs to cenſure the Meaſures of the Court, when he thought them wrong, as this Lord, and That the King did not like in a Servant.

On

On the Queen's Acceſſion to the Throne, he was diſmiſſed from all his Employments.

He is certainly one of the compleateſt Gentlemen in *England*, hath a very clear Underſtanding, and manly Expreſſions, with abundance of Wit. He is brave in his Perſon, much of a Libertine, of a middle Stature, fair Complexion, and fifty Years old.

The most Universal Villain I ever knew.

Charles,

Charles, Lord *Mohun*,

IS the Reprefentative of a very ancient Family, but had the Misfortune
to come to the Title young, while the
Eftate was in Decay; his Quality intro-
duced him into the beft Company, but
his Wants very often led him into bad;
fo that he became one of the arranteft
Rakes in Town, and indeed a Scandal
to the Peerage; was generally a Sharer
in all Riots; and before, he was twenty
Years old, was twice tried for Murther,
by the Houfe of Peers. On his being
acquitted at the laft Trial, he expreffed
his Confufion for the Scandal he brought
upon his Degree as a Peer by his Behaviour, in very handfom Terms, and
promifed to behave himfelf fo, for the
future, as not to give farther Scandal;
and he hath been as good as his Word;
for now he applies himfelf in good ear-
neft to the Knowledge of the Conftitution

tion of his Country, and to serve it ; and
having a great deal of fine and good Senfe,
turned this way, makes him very confiderable in the Houfe ; he is brave in his
Perfon, bold in his Expreffions, and
rectifies, as faft as he can, the Slips of his
Youth by Acts of Honefty; which he
now glories in more, than he was formerly extravagant; he was married when
very young, to a Niece of my Lord
Macclesfield; who dying without Iffue,
left him a confiderable Eftate, which he
well improves.

The Queen continues him Colonel
of a Regiment of Foot; he is of a middle Stature, inclining to fat, not thirty
Years old.

*e was little better than a Conceited
Sher in Company.*

Earl

Earl of *Kent*,

IS the firſt Branch of the Antient Family of *Grey*. The preſent Gentleman
was much eſteemed, when Lord *Ruthen*;
was always very moderate, has good
Senſe, and a good Eſtate; which, with
his Quality, muſt make him always bear
a conſiderable Figure in the Nation; he
is a handſome Man, not above forty
Years old. *He ſeems a good natur'd*
man but of very little conſequence

Earl of *Lindſey*,

IS the Repreſentative of the *Batties*,
handſome in his Perſon, of a fair
Complexion, doth not trouble himſelf
with Affairs of State; but, his Brother
is Vice Chamberlain, and a Privy
Counſellor, a fine Gentleman, has both
Wit and Learning.
I never obſerved a grain of either
Montagu

Montagu *Venables Bertie,* Earl of *Abingdon,*

IS a Branch of the *Berties*; a Gentleman of fine Parts, makes a good Figure in the Counties of *Oxford* and *Buckinghamſhire.* Was made by the Queen Conſtable of the *Tower* of *London*, is very high for the Monarchy and Church, of a black Complexion, paſt forty Years old. *very covetous.*

Philip Stanhope, Earl of *Cheſterfield,*

IS the Repreſentative of the *Stanhopes,* a good Family in *England*; he is very ſubtle and cunning, never entered into the Meaſures of King *William*, nor ever will, in all Probability, make any great Appearance in any other Reign. He is above ſixty Years old.

If it be old Cheſterfield, I have William heard He was the greateſt Knave in England.

William, Earl of *Yarmouth*,

OF the Name of *Paston* in *Norfolk*, was a Nonjuror all King *William*'s Reign, but a Man of Senfe and Knowledge in the Affairs of his Country; above fifty Years old.

Charles, Earl of *Berkeley*,

WAS Lord *Durfley*, Ambaffador from King *William* to the States of *Holland*, is a Gentleman of Learning, Parts, and a Lover of the Conftitution of his Country; a fhort fat Man, fifty Years old. *Intolerable lazy r h ge len and fomewhat covetous*

Robert Darcy, Earl of *Holdernefs*,

IS a very young Gentleman, hath been abroad in the World; a Lover of the Conftitution of his Country to a great Degree, of good Nature, fair Complexion, not thirty Years old.

H

Thom.1s,

Thomas, Earl of *Aylesbury,*

IS a Branch of the Antient Family of *Bruce* in *Scotland.* This Gentleman declared himself for King *James,* and is now abroad; does not want Sense, is very tall, fair Complexioned, past fifty Years old.

Earl of *Litchfield,*

IS of the Name of *Lee,* a Man of Honour, never could take the Oaths to King *William,* hath good Sense, is not yet come to Queen *Anne*'s Court, fifty Years old.

Earl of *Feversham,*

IS a third Son of the Family of *Duras* in *France*; he came over with one of the Duke of *York*'s Family; was made an Earl, had the Garter, and a Troop of Guards; was Lieutenant General of that Prince's Army, he took the Oaths to King *William,* and came to Parliament. He is a middle Statured brown Man, turned of fifty Years old.

He was a very dull old Fellow   Other

ther Windfor, Earl of *Plymouth.*

'S a handfom well made Man, of a
 fair Complexion; loves his Bottle
ıd Play; hath good Senfe when he pleaf-
:h to fhew it; is not thirty Years old.

Henry d'Auverquerque, Earl of *Grantham.*

[S Son to *Monfieur Auverquerque.* He
married the Duke of *Ormond's* Sifter.
Ie is a very pretty Gentleman, fair
Complexioned, and paft thirty Years old. *and
good for nothing.*

George, Lord *Abergaveney.*

I S Gentleman of the Bed-Chamber
 to the Prince of *Denmark,* hath
Learning, Wit, and one of the beft
Libraries in *England*; is a little brown
Man, very lovely, thirty Years old.

John, Lord *De la Warr*.

IS Groom of the Stole to the Prince
of *Denmark*, a good Family of the
Name of *Weſt*, and had its Beginning,
by making King *John* of *France* Priſoner in the Reign of King *Edward* the
Third. He was always attached to the
preſent Queen's Family; ſeldom waited
on King *William*; a free jolly Gentleman, turned of forty Years old. *of very*
la ſenſe, but formal tweche ſtockſſ with the
eſt kind of loweſt Pelticks.

Robert, Lord *Ferrers*.

IS a very honeſt Man, a Lover of his
Country, a great Improver of Gardening and Parking; a keen Sportſman,
never was yet in Buſineſs, but is very
capable; a tall, fair Man, towards ſixty
Years old.

William,

William, Lord *Paget.*

WAS Ambaſſador and Plenipotentiary at the Treaty of *Car-
witz*; is a very honeſt Gentleman, and
ealous for the Liberty of the People;
f good Intereſt in the Country, and
ipable of any Share in the Adminiſtra-
on. Is near ſixty Years old.

Robert, Lord *Lexington.*

IS of the Name of *Sutton,* was Gentle-
·man of the Horſe to the Princeſs
iow Queen) when the Difference hap-
ened between her and King *William*
nd left her Service; was made Gentle-
nan of the Bed-Chamber to the King,
nd ſent Envoy to the Court of *Vienna.*
Ie is of a good Underſtanding, and
iery capable to be in the Miniſtry; a
well bred Gentleman, and an agreeable
Companion; handſome, of a brown
Complexion; forty Years old.

Nevil,

Nevil, Lord *Lovelace.*

IS. Lieutenant Colonel of the Horse Guards, a very pretty Gentleman, of good Sense, and well at Court, a short, fat, brown Man, not forty Years old.

Charles, Lord *Howard* of *Escrick.*

IS brave in his Person; hath been under some unhappy Characters and Circumstances, which hath hindred his Advancement, both in the last Reign and This; he was against King *William's* Ministry, and takes all Occasions to shew it; very fair Complexioned, poor, past forty Years old.

Ford,

Ford, Lord *Grey* of *Werk.*

IS Brother to the late Earl of *Tanker-ville,* who having no Sons, this Gentleman fucceeded in the Title of *Grey* ; he was Governour of *Barbadoes,* under King *William,* and always well efteemed by that Prince, and is truly. a fweet difpofed Gentleman; he joined King *William* at the *Revolution,* and is a zealous Affertor of the Liberties of the People; a thin, brown, handfom Man, middle Stature, turned of forty Years old. *Had very little in him.*

James, Lord *Chandos.*

WAS warm againft King *William's* Reign, and doth not make any great Figure in this; but, his Son, Mr. *Bridges* * does, being a Member of the Houfe of Commons, one of the Coun-fellors to the Prince, and a very worthy Gentleman. *But a great Complier in whatever Court*

* The prefent Duke of *Chandos.*

H 4

Francis, Lord *Guilford*.

IS Son to the Lord Keeper *North*, hath been abroad, does not want Senſe nor Application to Buſineſs, and his Genius leads him that Way. The Queen made him Lord Lieutenant of *Eſſex*; he is fat, fair, of middle Stature, and paſt thirty Years o.d. *A Mighty Silly Fellow.*

John, Lord *Haverſham*.

WAS Sir *John Thomſon*, and made a good Figure, in the Houſe of Commons, moſt of King *William*'s Reign; on his being created a Peer, he was made one of the Lords of the Admiralty. He is very eloquent, but very paſſionate and fiery, a Diſſenter by Principle, and always turbulent. He is a ſhort red Faced Man, paſt fifty Years old.

Charles.

Charles, Lord *Cornwallis.*

IS a Gentleman of a sweet Disposition, a great lover of the Constitution, and well esteemed in his native County of *Suffolk*; inclining to Fat, fair Complexion, not Thirty Years old.

Thomas, Lord *Howard* of *Effingham.*

IS a very pretty, modest, young Gentleman; hath a great many good Things in him, not Twenty-five Years old.

Foulk

Foulk Grevil, Lord *Brook.*

HAth been always a Man of Pleafure, with a very good Capacity; well bred, loves Play, a fair Complexion, towards Sixty Years of Age.

His Son, Mr. *Grevil,* makes a tolerable Figure in the *Houfe of Commons:* Both great Affertors of the Prerogative in *Church* and *State.*

William, Lord *Craven.*

HAth a very good Eftate, loves Field-fports and a Bottle; is very fat, and fair; towards Forty Years old.

Lord *Griffin.*

HAving followed King *James's* Fortunes, is now in *France.* He was always a great Sportfman, and brave; a good Companion, turned of Sixty Years old. Lord

His fon was a plain Drunken Companion.

Lord *Cholmondeley*.

IS a Gentleman of a good Eftate in *Chefhire*, hath good Senfe, did not come much to King *William*'s Court ; but his Brother was made one of the Bed-chamber, and commands the Horfe-Granadiers. This Lord is a great Lover of Country Sports ; is hand-fom in his Perfon, and turned of Forty Years old. *Good for nothing as far as I ever knew.*

John, Lord *Afhburnham.*

HAth a great Eftate in *Suffex*, and improves it. Is a thin, brown Man, Fifty Years old.

John,

John, Lord *Harvey*.

IS a Gentleman of a very good Eftate in *Suffolk*, and was created a Peer by Queen *Anne*. He is a great Sportf-man, lover of Horfe-Matches and Play; made always a good Figure in the *Houfe of Commons* ; is zealous for the Laws and Liberties of the People ; a handfom Man in his Perfon, fair Complexion, middle Stature, Forty Years old.

John Cecil, Earl of *Exeter*.

IS a Gentleman who never was yet in Bufinefs ; loves *Hawking*, *Horfe-Matches*, and other Country Sports.

Scroop

Scroop Egerton, Earl of *Bridgwater.*

'S a very hopeful young Gentleman, hath been Abroad, is married to a daughter of the Duke of *Marlborough :* not Twenty-five Years old.

Thomas, Earl of *Suffex.*

'S of the Name of *Lennard,* wishes very heartily for the Welfare of his Country ; of no great Genius. Fifty Years old.

George

George Booth, Earl of Warrington.

IS Son to that famous Lord *Delamere*, who was Tried for Treason in King *James*'s Reign ; and was one of those who carried the Message from the Prince of *Orange*, to that Prince to depart from *Whitehall*, and was created Earl of *Warrington*. This Gentleman makes no great Figure in his Country, Parliament, or Person. Past Thirty Years old.

Lord *Butler* of *Weston*.

IS Earl of *Arran* in *Ireland*, and Brother to the Duke of *Ormond* : He commands a Troop of Horse-Guards ; was Gentleman of the Bed-chamber to King *William* ; of very good Sense, though seldom shews it. Of a fair Complexion, middle Stature, towards Forty Years old. *This is right, but he is the most negligent man of* Sir *his own affairs*

Sir *Edward Seymour*.

IS of a very good Family, and born to a good Eftate in the *Weſt* of *England* ; made a good Figure in the Reign of King *Charles* the Second, was Speaker of the *Houſe of Commons*, and Treaſurer of the *Navy*.

Was always fuſpected to be in the *French* Intereſt; and was Impeached by the Commons. At the *Revolution* he oppoſed King *William*'s coming to the Throne; but that Prince brought him over, by making him a Privy-Coun-fellor, and Lord of the *Treaſury*. He not anſwering the King's Expectation, was turned out, and during the reſt of that Prince's Reign, was at the Head of thoſe who oppoſed the Meaſures of the Court, in the *Houſe of Commons*. He was the zealouſeſt Man for Impeaching the *Partition* ; and the King made him

.Advan-

Advances on that Occafion, below his Dignity, calling a New Parliament, by his and my Lord *Rochefter's* Direction; and fquaring the Government by his Rule : But nothing being able to bring this Gentleman into hearty Meafures againft *France,* that Parliament was immediately Diffolved, and a new one called, when the King dyed.

On the Queen's Acceffion to the Throne, he was made Comptroller of the Houfhold, and of the Privy Council.

He is believed to be the prudenteft Man in *England*; of great Experience in the Affairs of his Country, but extremely carried away by Paffion; does not value Scandal; and was openly vifited by the *French* Ambaffador, when the People feemed to fufpect him in that Intereft.

He hath eftablifhed his Family very well, his *Second* Son being a Major-General

neral in the Army, and a Lieutenant in the Band of Penfioners; his *Third* Son is created a Peer, by the Title of Lord *Conway*; and the *Fourth* is Gentleman of the Bed-chamber to the Prince of *Denmark.*

He hath a very erect Countenance, and is a ftately Man for his Age; of a fair, fanguine Complexion, about Seventy Years old.

Since the writing of thefe Characters, he is turned out of all, and is fucceeded in his Place of Comptroller, by Mr. *Manfel.*

Mr.

Mr. *Manfel.*

IS a young Gentleman of a very good Eftate in *Wales*. He always made an agreeable Figure in the *Houfe of Commons* ; was generally an Oppo-fer of the Meafures of King *William's* Reign, yet was very civilly enter-tained by that Prince, in a Vifit he made him at *Loo* *, two Years before he died.

He is a Gentleman of a great deal of Wit and Good Nature, a lover of the Ladies, and a pleafant Companion : Is very thin, of a fair Complexion, mid-dle Stature, and turned of thirty Years old.

* King *William's* Palace in *Holland.*

—of good nature but of a very moderate capacity.

Robert

Robert Harley, Efq; Speaker of the *Houfe of Commons.*

IS a Gentleman of a good Family in *Herefordfhire*, who hath taken a great deal of Pains to underftand the Conftitution of his Country thoroughly. He was Active for the *Revolution*, but being mifunderftood at *Court*, and in the *Houfe of Commons*, he openly Voted againft the Principles he had always profeffed; when he faw the Court did not gratify him fo well as he thought he deferved; and though fome Steps were made towards gaining him to King *William*, yet he made no Advance, till that Parliament was called which impeached the *Partition*, to which he was chofen *Speaker*, as he was to That which fucceeded.

No Man underftands more the Management of that *Chair* to the Advantage of his Party, nor knows better all the

Tricks

Tricks of the House. He is skilled in moſt
Things, and very <u>Eloquent</u>; was bred
a *Presbyterian*, yet joins with the *Church-*
Party in every Thing; and they do nothing without him.

He would make a good *Chancellor*, or
Maſter of the Rolls: He is a very uſeful
Man, and for that Reaſon, is well with
the Miniſtry. He never fails to have
a *Clergyman* of each Sort at his Table
on *Sunday*; his Family go generally
to the *Meeting*.

He is of low Stature, and ſlender;
turned of Forty.

Since the writing of theſe *Charaſters*,
he is made *Secretary of State* in the
Room of my Lord *Nottingham*.

He could not properly be call'd Eloquent
but He knew how to prevail on the
with few Words & ſtrong reaſons

John

John Howe, Esq, Pay-master to the Army.

IS Younger Brother of Sir *Scroop Howe*, a good Family in *Nottinghamshire*; but this Gentleman settled in *Gloucestershire*, where, being chose a Member of Parliament, he soon made a good Figure in the *House of Commons.* He seemed to be pleased with, and joyned in the *Revolution*, and was made Vice-Chamberlain to Queen *Mary* ; but having asked a Grant, which was refused him, and given to my Lord *Portland*, he fell from the Court, and was all that Reign the most violent and open Antagonist King *William* had in the House. A great Enemy to Foreigners settling in *England*; most Clauses in Acts against Them, being brought in by him   He is indefatigable in whatever he undertakes; witness the *Old East-India Company*, whose Cause he maintained, 'till he fixed it upon as fure a Foot as the *New*, even when they thought themfelves paft Recovery.

He lives up to what his vifible Eftate can afford, and yet purchafes, inftead of running in Debt.

He is endued with good Natural Parts, attended with an unaccountable Boldnefs, daring to fay what he pleafes, and will be heard out; fo that he paffeth with fome for the *Shrew* of the Houfe

On the Queen's Acceffion to the Throne, he was made a Privy-Counfellor, and *Pay-mafter* of the *Guards* and *Garrifons*. He is a tall, thin, pale-faced Man, with a very wild Look ; brave in his Perfon, bold in expreffing himfelf, a violent Enemy, a fure Friend, and feems always to be in a Hurry. Near Fifty Years old.

Sir

Sir *George Rooke.*

IS of a Gentleman's Family in *Canterbury,* of no great Eftate, but always well efteemed in that County. He commanded a Ship at the *Revolution* ; and it is believed, if he had been in *England* when *that* happened, he would have been more Zealous for his Mafter King *James,* than moft of the *Proteftant* Captains were.

On the Recommendation of the *High-Church* Party, King *William* gave him a Flag, and a Penfion of a Thoufand Pounds a Year, which he enjoyed, notwithftanding the feveral Turns at Court. King *William* liked him for his Taciturnity, and his Readinefs to obey Orders, without Reafoning about them.

He was unfuccefsful in all the Expeditions wherein he commanded, except-

I 4

ing

ing that One, in forcing *Denmark* to make Peace with *Sweden* He commanded when the *French* deftroyed our *Turky*-Fleet at *Lagos-Bay*, and in that unhappy Expedition to *Cadiz* ; of which Mifcarriage he bears the Blame ; and had the *Gout* when he fhould have intercepted Count *Lagon*.

On the Queen's Acceffion to the Throne, he was made Admiral of the Fleet, and Vice-Admiral of *England*, and a Privy-Counfellor.

He is a Gentleman of very good Parts, fpeaks little, but to the Purpofe. He always fhewed a Diflike to Men of *Revolution-Principles*, and difcouraged them all he could in the Navy. He was warm in the *Houfe of Commons* for Impeaching the *Partition*; and, contrary to the King's Command, made a *Speech* which baulked Sir *Thomas Littleton's Speech*, then *Speaker*, when the King's Affairs required it

He

He maintains all his Ships with his Sword, and is ready enough to give any Man Satisfaction who queſtions his Conduct that Way. If he hath the Misfortune to do no Service, as yet, to his Country, he hath the Capacity to do a great deal, if he pleaſes to apply himſelf to it. He is a ſtern-looked Man, of a Brown Complexion, well Shaped, and Sixty Years old.

Sir *Cloudefly Shovell*.

OF very mean Parentage, born in a poor Village in *Norfolk*, was firſt Cabbin-Boy to Sir *John Narborough*, went with him in his Expedition, through the *Streights of Magellan*, to the *South-Sea*; paſſed through all the Degrees of a Sailor, and was made Captain of a Man of War in the Reign of King *Charles* the Second. He hath been a Flag-Officer all King *William*'s Reign, and is now Admiral of the *Blue*.

No Man underſtands the Affairs of the Navy better, or is beloved of the Sailors ſo well as he. He loves the *Conſtitution* of his *Country*, and ſerves it without any *factious Aim*; he married his Maſter *Narborough*'s Widow, and proves a very grateful Husband. He hath very good Natural Parts; familiar and plain in his Converſation; dreſſes without Affectation; a very large, fat, fair Man, turned of Fifty Years old.

James Vernon, Efq; Teller of the *Exchequer*.

WAS Clerk in the *Secretary's* Office in King *Charles* the Second's Reign; Secretary to the Duke of *Monmouth*; and, at the *Revolution*, was Under-Secretary to the Duke of *Shrewſbury* (then Secretary of *State*) in which Poſt he continued, as alſo Under-Secretary to *Trenchard*, and when the Duke came in a ſecond Time.

When *Lords Juſtices* were appointed to govern the Kingdom in the King's Abſence, he was made Secretary to that Commiſſion, and afterwards Secretary of State; in which Poſt he continued till the King died.

No Man underſtands all Parts of that great Office better than he, nor could manage it with ſo much Prudence, at

ſo

'ſo intricate a Time as the two laſt Ye:
of his Adminiſtration.

He was the Inſtrument made uſe
to accuſe the *Four* Lords for the P,
tition, who had all been his Benefacto
but he managed that Part with ſo mu
Fidelity to the King, who command
him to do it, and ſo much Fairneſs
the Lords accuſed, that it loſt him
Reputation.

His being made *Secretary* of *Sta*
without his Maſter the Duke of *Shrev*
bury's Knowledge, at a Time when t
Duke was ill uſed, ſurprized many, a
gave a Handle for his Enemies to {
hard Things of him ; but the Du
and his Friends are intirely ſatisfied, tl
he behaved himſelf with a great deal
Fidelity and Gratitude to his Gra
both when he was firſt *Clerk,* and wh
he was *Secretary* in conjunction w
him.

He is indefatigable in Bufinefs, and may be called a Drudge to the Office. , An ill Wife hath much foured his Temper, which makes him rougher in Bufinefs than could be expected from one of his Senfe and Experience ; but that Roughnefs is attended with fo much Candor, and is diftributed equally to all who have Bufinefs with him, that makes it the eafier borne. Never any *Secretary* of *State* wrote fo many Letters with his own Hand, as he, nor in a better Stile.

On the Queen's Acceffion to the Throne, her Majefty took the *Seals* from him, and gave them to my Lord *Nottingham* ; but to fhew, that it was not out of any diflike to his Service, made him *Teller* of the *Exchequer.*

He is a tall, thin Man, Brown complexioned, with an *Auftrian* Lip, a good Eye, carelefs in his Drefs, and rough in his Behaviour ; turned of fixty Years old.

Mr. *Boyle*, Chancellor of the *Exchequer*.

IS Brother to the Earl of *Burlington* and has been for many Years Representative for the University of *Cambridge* in Parliament : Is a good Companion in Conversation; agreeable amongst the Ladies ; serves the Queen very assiduously in Council ; makes a considerable Figure in the *House* of *Commons* by his prudent Administration, obliges every Body in the *Exchequer* ; and in Time may prove a Great Man.

He is of middle Stature, inclining to Fat, dark Complexion, wears his own Hair, and turned of Thirty Years old.

[handwritten: had some very scurvy Tricks; particular avarice]

S

Sir *Charles Hedges*, Secretary of State.

IS' of a good Family in *Wiltſhire*, bred a Civilian, was Judge Advocate for trying the Affair of *Magdalen* College in King *James's* Reign; was Knighted and made Judge of the Admiralty by King *William*.

When that Parliament was called, which impeached the *Partition*; he was made Secretary of State, and on its Diſſolution turned out.

On the Queen's Acceſſion to the Throne, the Seals were taken from my Lord *Mancheſter,* and reſtored to him again.

He is a better Companion, than a Stateſman; which proves very uſeful to
that

that Miniſtry which employs him, I
ing very zealous and induſtrious
his Party; he doth not want Ser
hath a very good Addreſs in Bu
neſs, is a handſom Man, of a da
Complexion, turned of Forty-five Ye
old.

Sir *Thomas* Frankland, Poſt-Maſter General.

IS Chief of a very good Family in *Yorkſhire*, with a very good Eſtate; his being my Lord *Falconberg's* Nephew, and marrying a Grand-Daughter of *Oliver Cromwell*, firſt recommended him to King *William*, who, at the *Revolution*, made him Commiſſioner of the *Exciſe*, and in ſome Years after, Governour of the *Poſt-Office*; by abundance of Application, he underſtands that Office better than any Man in *England*. And as we lately had no Intercourſe with *France* but War, improved that Revenue to ſome thouſand Pounds a Year more, than it was in the moſt flouriſhing Years; He was the firſt that erected a Correſpondence with *Spain*, *Portugal*, and all our foreign Plantations, to the great advantage of our Trade; and is known by your

K.   *Wigan*

Matters, when the Government {
think fit to employ him. The Que
by Reafon of his great Capacity and I
nefty, hath continued him in the Of
of Pay-Mafter General.

He is a Gentleman of a very fw
eafy, affable Difpofition; of good Ser
extreme zealous for the Conftitution
his Country, yet does not feem over {
ward; keeps an exact Unity amor
the Officers under him, and encoura
them in their Duty, thro' a peculiar
miliarity, by which he obliges them, a
keeps up the Dignity of being Mafl

He is a handfom Man, middle S
ture, towards forty Years old.

A fair Character

Mr. *Smith*, one of her Majesty's Privy Council.

IS a Gentleman of a good Estate in *Hampshire*, made a very considerable Figure in the *House* of *Commons*, all King *William*'s Reign, was a Lord of the Treasury, and Chancellor of the Exchequer; but on Impeaching the *Partition*, quitted his Employments.

On the Queen's Accession to the Throne, he was continued a Privy Counsellor, and often called. He is a Gentleman of much Honour, a Lover of the Constitution of his Country; a very agreeable Companion in Conversation, a bold Orator in the *House* of *Commons* †, when the Interest of his Country is at Stake; of a good Address, middle Stature, fair Complexion, turned of forty Years old.

† He was Speaker.

K 2   *Charles*

I thought him a heavy Man.

Charles D'Avenant, L. L. D.

IS Son of Sir *William D'Avenant,* the Poet; bred up to the Civil Law; in the Reign of King *James,* he was made a *Commiſſioner* of the *Exciſe,* but turned out at the *Revolution,* although by a Book, which he then wrote, he ſeemed to underſtand that Branch of the Revenue very well; he made ſeveral Advances to the Miniſtry in King *William's* Time; but to no Purpoſe; their Neglect and his Poverty ſoured him to that Degree, as to prove the greateſt Scourge they had, and the greateſt Inſtrument to leſſen them with the People; his Book on *Trade,* and its *Ballance;* when they were ſetting up a new *Faſt India Company,* his Treatiſe on *Grants,* and *Reſumptions,* when the Parliament recalled thoſe in *Ireland* ; and, his *Collection* of *Treaties* at the *Partition,* are ſo many Libels on the Miniſtry, · his *Dialogue* between *Whig-*

love.

love and *Double,* calculated for the mean-
eſt Capacity, gave a Sparring-Blow, in
the Country, which was viſible in the
Elections for the Parliament, that was
then choſen ; he hath been of the *Houſe*
of *Commons* ſeveral Seſſions, but never
made any Figure ; his Talent lay more
in Writing than Speaking.

On the Queen's Acceſſion to the
Throne, he was made Secretary to the
Union with *Scotland*; his Son was ſent
Reſident to *Frankfort,* and himſelf after-
wards made Inſpector General.

He was very poor at the *Revolution,*
had no Buſineſs to ſupport him all the
Reign of King *William,* yet made a good
Figure.

He is a very cloudy-looked Man, fat,
of middle Stature, about fifty Years old.

He was lived ill by most Princes
He ruined his own Estate, with paying his
the necessity of K 3 *complying with the*
Matthew

Matthew Prior, Eſq; Com-miſſioner of Trade.

WAS taken from the Bar of a Ta-vern by my Lord *Corſet*, and ſent to the Univerſity of *Cambridge*; was Contemporay with *Montague* Lord *Hali-fax*, and joined with him in writing that fine Satire againſt Mr. *Dryden*, called, *The* Hind *and* Panther *tranſvers'd, to the Story of the* City Mouſe *and* Country Mouſe.

At the *Revolution* he was brought to Court, and ſent to *Holland*, as Secretary to my Lord *Durſley*; and after that Lord's being recalled, was continued Secretary for the *Engliſh* Nation to the States Ge-neral for ſome Years.

When my Lord *Jerſey* was made one of the Lords Juſtices in *Ireland*, he was made Secretary to that Commiſſion;

as

as also to the Treaty of *Ryswijck*, and to the Lords *Portland* and *Jersy*, Ambassadors in *France*, and afterwards one of the Commissioners of Trade.

He was chosen a Member of that Parliament which Impeached the *Partition*, to this *Treaty* he was Secretary, and yet joined in the *Vote* with Those who carried on the Impeachment against Those that had established him in the World.

On the Queen's Accession to the Throne, he was continued in his Office, is very well at Court with the Ministry, and is an intire Creature of my Lord *Jersey*'s, whom he supports by his Advice. Is one of the best Poets in *England*, but very factious in Conversation; a thin hollow-looked Man, turned of forty Years old.

This is near the truth.

Thomas,

Thomas, Archbifhop of *Canterbury*, is

DR. *Tenifon*; he was made Rector of the Parifh of St. *Martin's* in the Fields, in the Reign of King *Charles* the Second; was always a Man of moderate Principles, and a great Oppofer of the Progrefs of Popery in the Reign of King *James*: His Moderation brought him to the Bifhoprick of *Lincoln*, by King *William*; and Dr. *Tillotfon's* Death, to be Archbifhop of *Canterbury*.

He is a plain, good, heavy Man, now much in Years, and wearing out; very tall, of a fair Complexion, and feventy Years old.

The most good for nothing Prelate I ever knew.

John,

John, Archbishop of *York,* is

DR. *Sharp,* he was Rector of St. *Giles's* in the Fields, in the Reign of King *James*; when, preaching warmly against Popery, he was filenced, and the Bishop of *London* (Dr. *Compton*) fufpended from his Office, for not turning him out.

He was made by King *William* Archbishop of *York*; and this Queen hath made him her Lord Almoner.

He is one of the greateft Ornaments of the Church of *England*, of great Piety and Learning; a Llack Man, and fifty-five Years old.

Gilbert,

Gilbert, Biſhop of *Salisbury*.

IS of a very good Family in *Scotland*, of the Name of *Burnet*, his Father was *laid* Lord of *Cremont*.

This Gentleman was Profeſſor of Divinity, in the Univerſity of *Glaſgow*, and Chaplain to Duke *Hamilton*; as a Compliment to which Family, he wrote the *Memoirs of the two laſt Dukes*; but his making his Addreſs to the Duke's Niece, a Daughter of the Earl of *Caſſilis*, he was obliged, upon the Diſcovery, to run away with her to *England*; where he married her; and changed Sides; running into the Duke of *Lauderdale*'s Party, who advanced him to be Chaplain of the Rolls; but having preached with ſome freedom againſt the prevailing Popiſh Party, he was obliged alſo to leave *England*.

He

He travelled fome Years into *Italy,*
nd printed, in Letters, his Defcriptions
f that Country. Married again in
Iolland, came over with King *William*.
t the *Revolution,* and was made Bifhop
f *Salisbury.*

He is one of the greateft Orators of *Scot*
he Age he lives in. His *Hiftory of the*
Reformation, and his *Expofition of the*
Thirty-Nine Articles, fhew him to be a
Man of great Learning ; but feveral of
iis other Works fhew him to be a
Man neither of Prudence nor Temper ;
iis fometimes oppofing, and fome-
imes favouring, the *Diffenters,* hath
nuch expofed him to the Generality
f the People of *England;* yet he is
ery ufeful in the *Houfe* of *Peers,* and
roves a great Pillar, both of the Civil
nd Ecclefiaftical Conftitution, againft
he Incroachments of a Party which
rould deftroy Both.

*His true Character woud take up too mu
tme for me (who knew him well) to
wriba?*

On the Queen's Acceſſion to the Throne, he was the firſt who brought the News to her of King *William*'s Death, and ſaluted her Queen; yet was turned out of his Lodgings at Court, and met with ſeveral Affronts.

He is a large, bold-looked Man, ſtrong made, and turned of Fifty Years old.

N. B. *For a farther Account of this* Prelate, *ſee his* Will, &c. *in the* Appendix, *Numb.* I.

CHA-

CHARACTERS

Of the ENGLISH

Foreign Minifters.

George Stepney, Efq; Envoy Extraordinary to the Emperor.

IS defcended from the Family of the *Stepneys* in *Pembrokefhire*, but was born in *Weftminfter*; had his Education in theUniverfity of *Cambridge*, at the fame Time with Mr. *Montague*, now Lord *Halifax*; was by him brought to Town, and fent *Secretary* to Mr. *Johnftoun*, Envoy at *Berlin*; and when that Gentleman was recalled to be *Secretary* of State for *Scotland*, Mr. *Stepney* continued

nued in the Bufinefs at Berlin, was made Refident, and in fome Time after was fent Envoy to the King of *Poland*, and other *German* Princes; which Commiffions he difcharged fo well, that on his Return to *England*, the King made him one of the *Commiffioners* of *Trade*, and fent him to refide as Envoy Extraordinary at the Court of *Vienna*, where the *Queen* continues him.

No *Englishman* ever underftood the Affairs of *Germany* fo well, and few *Germans* better.

He is a Gentleman of admirable Natural Parts, very Learned, one of the beft Poets now in *England*, and, perhaps, equal to any that ever was; hath an admirable, clear, Stile in his Letters; of very good, diverting, Converfation; a thorough Statefman, fpeaks all the Modern Languages, as well as Antient, perfectly well. Is a fhort Man in Stature, with a pleafant Countenance, towards forty Years old.

Mr. *Methuen*, Ambaſſador to the King of *Portugal*.

WAS bred a Common Lawyer, and hath been many Years employed in the Affairs of *Portugal*, which he underſtands perfectly well.

In King *William*'s Reign he was made Lord Chancellor of *Ireland*, and was once very near being So in *England*.

He is a Man of Intrigue, but very muddy in his Conceptions, and not quickly underſtood in any Thing. In his Complexion and Manners, much of a *Spaniard*; a tall, Black Man, Fifty Years old..

A proſligate Rogue, without Religion or Morals, but cunning enough, yet without Abilitys of any kind.

Mr.

Mr. *Vernon*, Envoy to the King of *Denmark*.

IS Son of Mr. Secretary *Vernon*, Teller of the *Exchequer*; a young Gentleman, who hath had a fine Education; is Master of abundance of Learning; is very modest and sober, speaks little, not twenty-five Years old.

John Robinson, Esq; Resident in *Sweden*,

WAS bred a Clergyman, and hath lived so long at *this Court*, that it is not to be supposed any body can understand the Affairs of the Kingdom better. In his Deportment, and every Thing else, a *Swede*; of good Sense, grave, sober, and very careful in his Business. About Fifty Years old.*

* He wrote an Account of *Sweden*; was one of the Privy-Council to Queen *Anne*; and First Plenipotentiary of the Congress at *Utrecht*, 1712. Died Bishop of *London*.

Lord

Lord *Raby*, Envoy Extraordinary to the King of *Pruſſia*.

IS a Gentleman of the Name of *Went-worth*, and of the Family of *Strafford* ; he was Page to King *James's* Queen ; and, after the *Revolution*, was made Groom of the Bed-chamber to King *William*, with whom he was in great Favour.

On my Lord *Strafford's* Death, he ſucceeded in the Title of *Raby-Caſtle*, and the Peerage ; was ſent into *France* with my Lord *Portland*, and Envoy from King *William* to the King of *Pruſſia*.

On the Queen's Acceſſion to the Throne, the King of *Pruſſia* ſhewed his Inclinations to have the ſame Gentleman, upon which, her Majeſty again ſent him her Envoy to that Court.

L   He

He is a young Gentleman, *de bon Naturel*, handſom, of fine Underſtanding, and, with Application, may prove a Man of Buſineſs.

He is of low Stature, well-ſhaped, with a good Face, fair Complexioned, not thirty Years old.

Mr. *Hill,* Envoy Extraordinary to the Duke of *Savoy* *.

IS a Gentleman of a good Family in *Shropshire.* He was defigned for the Church, and took <u>Deacon</u>'s Orders; but having a Genius for Bufinefs, and falling into the Acquaintance of my Lord *Ranelagh,* when Tutor to my Lord *Hyde,* he was fent into *Flanders* as Pay-mafter to the *Englifh* Troops there, during the laft War.

He acquitted himfelf with great Reputation in this Poft, efpecially when our Money was bad; preventing, by his Conduct, the Army's Mutinying for want of Pay, a whole Campaign together; and had great Credit with the *Dutch.*

* i. e. *Victor Amadeus* II. late King of *Sardinia,* who, *Anno* 1730, refigned the Crown in Favour of his Son *Charles Emanuel*; but, attempting to refume it, is now, 1732, confined in the Caftle of *Rivole.* A fhort *Hiftory* of his *Abdication* is made publick.

He

He was Envoy at *Bruſſels* to the Duke of *Bavaria,* on the Concluſion of the Peace of *Ryſwijk,* ſent to the Court of *Savoy,* and, on his Return to *England,* made one of the Lords of the Treaſury; in which Poſt he continued all the King's Reign.

On the Queen's Acceſſion to the Throne, my Lord *Godolphin* being made Lord High Treaſurer, Mr. *Hill* was made one of the Council to the Prince, in his Office of Lord High Admiral; and, on the Duke of *Savoy*'s declaring for the Emperor, was ſent Envoy from *England* to *Turin.*

He is a Gentleman of very clear Parts, and affects Plainneſs and Simplicity in his Dreſs, and Converſation eſpecially. He is a Favourite to both Parties, and is beloved for his eaſy Acceſs, and affable Way by thoſe he has Buſineſs to do with. He is a thin, tall Man, taller than the ordinary Stature, near Fifty Years old.   Sir

Sir *Lambert Blackwell*, Envoy to the Great Duke of *Tuscany*,

IS Son to a Gentleman of *Ireland*, who was Manager of the Revenue, in the Time of *Oliver Cromwell*, and Grandson to General *Lambert* ; was bred a Merchant, and lived as such many Years at *Leghorn*. His long Acquaintance with the Court of *Florence*, and his Knowledge in the Affairs of *Italy*, first recommended him to King *William*, who made him Envoy to this Duke, and to the State of *Genoa*, at the Time when the *Partition* was in Agitation.

He affects much the Gentleman in his Dress, and the Minister in his Conversation : Is very lofty, yet courteous, when he knows his People ; much envied by his Fellow Merchants ; of a sanguine Complexion, taller than the ordinary Size, about Forty Years old.

He seem'd a very good Natur'd Man.

L 3

Sir *Robert Sutton*, Ambaſſador to the *Grand Seignior*.

HE is a near Relation to my Lord *Lexington*, and was bred a *Churchman*. He went to *Vienna* with that Lord, in the Capacities both of *Chaplain* and *Secretary*. He was left to do the Buſineſs at that Court when my Lord *Lexington* was recalled.

He was afterwards ſent Ambaſſador to the *Ottoman* Port, by this Queen : Is a young Gentleman of good Senſe, with a fair Complexion, and turned of thirty Years old.

Mr.

Mr. *Stanhope*, Envoy Extraordinary to the *States General* of the *United Provinces*,

IS of the Family of *Chesterfield*. His great Experience in Foreign Negotiations, makes him one of the best Ministers we have. He is a Man of Honour, and understands all the Punctilio's of Business and Conversation, and pleases the *Dutch*.

His Son, Colonel *Stanhope*, is one of the finest young Gentlemen we have; is very learned, with a great deal of Wit. King *William* designed to have sent him to the Court of *Sweden*; and he is certainly fit for any Negotiation, the Father is now old, and the Son a handsom black Man, turned of thirty Years of Age.

Mr.

Mr. *Pooley*, Envoy to the Court of *Hanover*,

IS of a very antient and good Family in the County of *Suffolk*; he was sent, at the *Revolution*, Envoy to the Duke of *Savoy*; but not pleasing that Court, was recalled, and was no more employed all King *William*'s Reign.

The Queen sent him to succeed Mr. *Cresset* at the Court of *Hanover*; he is a well bred Gentleman, with good Sense and Learning, fair Complexioned, thin, towards fifty Years old.

Mr

Mr. *Aglionby*, Envoy to the *Swifs-Cantons*.

IS the Son of a Clergyman in *Cum-berland*, and was bred to the Civil Law ; in which Profeffion having but fmall Encouragement, Mr. *Frowde* took him into the Poft Office, and made him *Language-Secretary*; but at the Revolution he helped to turn Mr. *Frowde* out; was fent into *Spain* to fettle the Pofts betwixt *England* and that Kingdom; and from thence went with a Commiffion as Envoy to *Turin*. On the Conclufion of the Peace of *Ryfwijk*, he was fent into *France*, to fettle the Intercourfe of Letters; and on the Queen's Acceffion to the Throne, was taken by my Lord *Nottingham* into his Office, and afterwards fent Envoy to *Switzerland*.

He hath abundance of Wit, and underftands moft of the modern Languages

Ireland, and Governour of the Ifle of *Wight;* had the fecond Regiment of Foot Guards, and was made a Major-General.

On the Queen's Acceffion to the Throne, he was made a Lieutenant General of the Forces in *Holland;* he hath abundance of Wit, but too much feized with Vanity and Self-conceit; he is affable, familiar, and very brave. Few confiderable Actions happened in this as well as the laft War, in which he was not, and hath been wounded in all the Actions where he ferved; is efteemed to be a mighty vigilant Officer, and for putting the Military Orders in Execution; he is pretty tall, lufty, well fhaped, and an agreeable Companion; hath great Revenues, yet fo very expenfive, as always to be in Debt; towards fifty Years old.

The vainest old fool alive

Lord

Lord *Teviot,* Lieutenant General,

WAS born in *Holland,* of *Scots* Parents, and came over a Lieutenant Colonel of Foot at the *Revolution*; had a Regiment of Dragoons given him in *Scotland*; afterwards, had the Command, in Chief, of the Forces in that Kingdom, and was made a Peer.

He is a Gentleman of a good Head, and underſtands moſt Things very well; hath purchaſed a greater Eſtate than any ſoldier in the King's Reign.

On the Queen's Acceſſion to the Throne, he was diſmiſſed from being Privy Counſellor and Commander in Chief, but continued in his Regiment of Dragoons. He is of a fair Complexion, fine ſhape, and well looked Man, towards fifty-five Years old.

Sir

Sir *Henry Bellasis*, Lieutenant General,

IS of a good Family in *Yorkshire*, and hath been long in the Army; but being accused of encouraging the Plunder of *Porta Santa Maria* in *Spain*, was broke; he makes a good Figure in the House of Commons, and would make one in the Country too, if he was not so very covetous.

He is a tall, handsom, sanguine complexioned Man, turned of fifty Years old.

Lieutenant General *Churchill,*

[S.Brother to the Duke of *Marlborough;* was Page to the late King of *Den-,ark,* and commanded in the Army ever .nce; he hath been always of Prince *ieorge*'s Bed-Chamber; and on the Jueen's Acceffion to the Throne, was nade Lieutenant of the *Tower* of *London.*

He is a good Bottle-Companion, hath Nit, is very brave, but very lewd; hath)een handfom, but now much battered; all, thin, and fifty Years old.

Lieutenant General *Earle,*

IS a Gentleman of a good Family and good Eftate in the Weft of *England.* Raifed a Regiment of Foot at the *Revolution,* and attended King *William* all his . Campaigns; was made, by the Queen, Commander in Chief of all the Forces in *Ireland*; has very good Senfe; a hearty Man for his Country, is brave, and loves his Bottle, turned of fifty Years old.

Lord

Lord *Gallway*, Lieutenant General,

IS Son to *Monsieur Rouvigny*, who was Ambassador from the *French* Court to King *Charles* the Second; had a Regiment of Horse given him at the *Revolution*, was sent to command under the Duke of *Savoy* the last War; and on that Prince's making Peace with *France*, was sent Commander in Chief to *Ireland*, and created a Peer.

He is one of the finest Gentlemen in the Army, with a Head fitted for the Cabinet, as well as the Camp; is very modest, vigilant, and sincere; a Man of Honour and Honesty; without Pride or Affectation; wears his own Hair, is plain in his Dress and Manners, towards sixty Years old.

all di:
etty
irwise

A deceitfull Hypocritical Factious Knave, a damnable Hypocrite of no Religion

David,

David, Lord *Portmore*, Lieutenant General,

IS Son of Sir *James Colyear*, who commanded a *Scots* Regiment in the States of *Holland*'s Service; came over Lieutenant Colonel of Foot, had a Regiment given him, and served all the last War, first in *Ireland*, and then in *Flanders*, with great Reputation.

On the Queen's Accession to the Throne, he was sent with the Duke of *Ormond* to *Cadiz*, and is now in *Spain*, being a Lieutenant General of Foot.

He is one of the best Foot Officers in the World; is very brave and bold, hath a great deal of Wit; very much a Man of Honour, and nice that way; yet married the Countess of *Dorchester*, and had by her a good Estate; pretty well shaped, dresses clean, has but one Eye, towards fifty Years old.

M

Lieu-

Lieutenant General *Wyndham*,

IS of a good Family, and hath been long in the Horſe Service in *England*. A very honeſt Gentleman, a good Companion, tall and thin, has but one Arm, is towards ſixty Years old.

Earl of *Orkney*, Lieutenant General,

IS a fourth Son of the late Duke *Hamilton*, and Brother to the Preſent; he was bred under his Uncle my Lord *Dumbarton*, who died in *France*; and after the *Revolution*, had his Regiment. He is a very well ſhaped black Man; is brave, but, by reaſon of a Heſitation in his Speech wants Expreſſion. Married Mrs. *Villiers*, and got a good Eſtate by her; is turned of forty Years old.

An honeſt good Natured Gentleman that hath much diſtinguiſhd himſelf as a Soldier

Lieu-

IS one of the Noble Family of *Lumley*, and Brother to the prefent Earl of *Scarborough*; hath ferved long in the Horfe, and is a good Officer, brave, but hot and paffionate to a great Degree; a Man of Honour. He is tall, fair, and forty-five Years old.

Sir *Charles Haro*, Lieutenant General,

WAS Tutor to the Earl of *Offory*, the Duke of *Ormond*'s Father, and had a Company in his Regiment in *Holland*. At the *Revolution* he had a Company in the Foot Guards; was afterwards Lieutenant Colonel to that Regiment; was made Colonel to the Fuzileers, and gradually advanced to the Poft he now hath, which he well deferves, being of good Underftanding, and abundance of Learning; fit to command, if not too covetous; he is a fhort, black Man, fifty Years old.　　M 2　　　Lieu-

His Father was a Groom; He was a man of Senfe; —— one grain of honefty

Lieutenant General *Ramſay*,

IS younger Son to the Earl of *Dal-houſy* in *Scotland*; he hath been bred up in *Holland*, came over at the *Revolution* with King *William*, commanded a Regiment of Foot, and had afterwards the Foot Guards of the Kingdom of *Scotland*.

On the Queen's Acceſſion to the Throne, he was made Commander in Chief of the Forces in that Kingdom. He is a Gentleman of a great deal of Fire, and very brave; of a ſanguine Complexion, well ſhaped; a thorough Soldier, and towards fifty Years old.

Colonel *Matthew Aylmer* *, Vice Admiral of the Fleet,

WAS Page to the Duke of *Bucking-ham*, and by him was fent a Re-formade to Sea; he commanded a Ship in the Reign of King *James*; and after the Engagement of *La Hogue*, (wherein Rear Admiral *Carter* was killed) he was made Rear Admiral; he was afterwards fent to the Mediterranean, where he gained a great deal of Reputation by the Treaties he concluded at *Algiers*, *Tunis* and *Tripoli*.

On the Queen's Acceffion to the Throne, becaufe he would not ferve under Colonel *Churchill*, he was difmiffed from all his Employments.

* Now Lord *Aylmer*,

M 3   He

He hath a very good Head, indefat
gable and defigning; is very zealous fc
the Liberties of the People, makes
good Figure in the Parliament, as we
as the Fleet; is handfom in his Perfoi
a brown Man, turned of fifty Yea
old.

Color

---

olonel *Churchill*, Vice Admiral,

'S Brother to the Duke of *Marl*
borough; in the Reign of *King*
arles the Second, he commanded a
ip; and in the Reign of *King James*
d King *William*, till the Affair of
Hogue, where, *Aylmer* being a Rear
fore him notwithstanding he was only
her Captain the [...], and [...]
ent into the Service of their Kings.

[illegible faded paragraph]

Sir *David Mitchell*, Vice Admiral,

WAS born in a little Fisher Town in *Scotland*, and was pressed into the *English* Service, when but a Boy: He hath past through all the Degrees of a Sailor, and without any Recommendation, but his own Merits, hath raised himself to the honourable Post he now enjoys, and had risen faster had he been an *Englishman*.

He taught Admiral *Russel*, now Lord *Orford*, Navigation; and it is to this Gentleman that his Lordship owes in a great Measure his Knowledge of Naval Affairs.

King *William*, besides his Preferment at Sea, created him Usher of the Black-Rod; and on the Queen's Accession to the Throne, he was continued in all his
                                                              Posts,

Posts, and was made one of the Council to the Prince, in his Office of Lord High Admiral.

He is a very just, worthy Man, of good solid Sense, but extremely afflicted with the Spleen, which makes him troublesome to others, as well as himself; he was the Author of that commendable Order, in the Navy, of preferring the Officers according to their Seniority, which takes off the powerful Sollicitations of great Men for Commands, for their Creatures, greatly to the Prejudice of the Service.

He is a fat sanguine Complexioned Man, turned of sixty Years old.

Marquis

Marquis of *Carmarthen**, Vice Admiral,

IS eldeſt Son of the Duke of *Leeds*; and underſtands all the Parts of a Sailor well; but is very rakiſh, and extravagant, in his manner of living, otherwiſe he had riſen quicker; he is ſtrong and active, with abundance of Fire, and does not want Wit; he is bold enough to undertake any Thing.

He contrived and built a Ship, called the *Royal Tranſport*, which proves ſo good a Sailor, that it ſhews his Knowledge of that Part of Navigation alſo; he is of a low Stature, but very well ſhaped, and ſtrong made, tho' thin; fair Complexioned, towards fifty Years old.

* Late Duke of *Leeds*.

Sir

Sir *Stafford Fairborne*, Vice Admiral,

IS Son of Sir *Palmes Fairborne*, who was Governour of *Tangier*, where this Gentleman was born; he hath had his Education, from a Boy, at Sea.

He is very brave, much of a Man of Honour, loves Play and a Bottle a little; hath good Senfe, is fat, fwarthy, of a moorifh Complexion, towards fifty Years old.

Sir *John Munden*, Vice Admiral,

WAS bred a Waterman; paſt all the Degrees of a Sailor, and was much eſteemed, till being ſent to the Coaſt of *Spain*, to intercept *Du Caſſe* at *Corunna*, his Neglect of that Affair brought him into Diſgrace; he was tried and acquitted by a Court Martial; yet her Majeſty taking the Examination of this Affair to herſelf, diſcharged him from all his Employments; he is a very plain Man in his Converſation and Dreſs, of a fair Complexion, towards ſeventy Years old.

Sir *Thomas Hopson*, Rear Admiral,

IS an old Sailor, yet never came to be higher than a Captain, till Sir *George Rooke*'s Expedition to the *Baltick*; he forced the Bomb at *Vigo*, and by his Conduct and Courage, was the great Instrument of that glorious Victory; for which the Queen knighted him, made him a confiderable Prefent, and confti- uted him one of the Commiſſioners of the Navy; and it is believed he is fo well pleafed with his laft Action, that he makes it his *ne plus ultra*, and will go to Sea no more; he is a fair Complexi- oned Man, towards fixty Years old.

Rear Admiral *Graydon,*

HATH ferved long at Sea; commanded a *Second* Rate in the Reign of King *William,* and was broke on Sufpicion of Cowardice, *&c.*

This Queen, on her Acceffion to the Throne, made him Rear Admiral, and fent him to command in the *Weft-Indies;* but meeting *Du Cape* in his Way, and not fighting him, and committing feveral Diforders in the *Plantations,* he was again difgraced, and turned out of all.

He is a vain bluftering bold Fellow, but makes more noife than brave Men generally do; affects the Tarr in his manner; a lufty Man; fifty Years old.

Rear

Rear Admiral *Byng* *,

IS one of the beſt Sailors in *England,* and a fine Gentleman in every Thing elſe; of a good Family and Eſtate in *Bedfordſhire,* underſtands all the ſeveral Branches of the Navy thoroughly; is a fair Complexioned Man, and towards fifty Years old.

* Now Earl of *Torrington.*

Rear Admiral *Wiſhart,*

WAS born in *Scotland,* and came over with King *William* at the *Revolution* in. a very ordinary Capacity: By great Application he hath raiſed himſelf to what he now is. He is a cloſe, prudent Man, underſtands the Sea very well; reckoned a Diſſenter, and is a great Patron of that Faction in the Fleet.

He hath had great luck in Prizes, and purchaſed a good Eſtate; he is a black Man, towards fifty Years old.

CHA

continued in both thefe Employments: But not being able to carry on Affairs in the Parliament of that Kingdom; and being accufed of endeavouring to create a Mifunderftanding betwixt the Queen and her Subjects, by a fham Plot, which had almoft fet the Parliament of *England* together by the Ears; he was difcharged from his Employments. He is a Gentleman of a good Eftate, a fine natural Difpofition, but apt to be influenced by People about him; hath a genteel Addrefs, much the manner of a Man of Quality, of eafy Accefs, thin, of a black Complexion, turned of forty-five Years old.

arl of *Seafield*, Lord High
Chancellor.

'S a younger Son of the Earl of *Fin-
later*, a branch of the Name of *Ogil-
e*, a good Family in *Scotland*; this
ntleman was bred to the Law, and
the *Revolution* was chosen Member of
: *Convention* of *States*, when he zea-
usly opposed the Throne vacant.

When Mr. *Johnstoun* was Secretary of
ate, he brought him over to King
illiam's Party, and made him Sollici-
r General of that Kingdom; then
inging him up to *London*, he made
; Court so effectually, that upon Mr.
hnstoun's and my Lord *Stair*'s Dismissi-
, he was made Secretary of State; in
uch Post he continued all King *Wil-
m*'s Reign; and upon the Queen's
cession to the Throne, was, from
retary of State, made Lord High

N 3   Chan-

Chancellor, and Knight Companion of the *Thiftle*.

He is a Gentleman of great Knowledge in the Civil Law, and the Conftitution of *that Kingdom;* underftands perfectly well how to manage the *Scots Parliament,* to the Advantage of the Court. That, and his implicitly executing what pleafed King *William,* without ever reafoning about it, eftablifhed him very much in his Majefty's Favour, but his joining with an *Englifh* Secretary, to deftroy the Colony of *Darien,* loft him extremely with the People.

He affects Plainnefs, and Familiarity in his Converfation, but is not fincere; is very beautiful in his Perfon, with a graceful Behaviour, a fmiling Countenance, and a foft Tongue, not forty Years old.

Duke

Duke of *Athol*, Lord Privy Seal,

IS the Reprefentative of the Noble Family of *Murray*; his Father the Marquis of *Athol* declared for King *James* at the *Revolution*: But this Gentleman declared for King *William*, and had a Regiment given him, and was created (his Father being ftill alive) Earl of *Tullibardin*, and made Secretary of State with *Seafield*; but the King having promifed an Employ in *Scotland* to fome Friend of his, for a confiderable Service he was to do in the *Scots* Parliament, and not performing his Promife; this Lord threw up the Seals, alledging that he could not juftify his Word given to his Friend any other Way.

On the Queen's Acceffion to the Throne, he was made Lord Privy Seal; and his Father dying, he was from Mar-

N 4   quis

quis made Duke of *Athol*, and Knight
Companion of the *Thistle*.

He is of a very proud, fiery, partial
Difposition; does not want Senfe, but
choaks himfelf with Paffion; which he
is eafily wound up to, when he fpeaks
in publick Affemblies, where his Quality always makes him heard; he hath
five Brothers, of whom two are Peers;
the Earl of *Dunmore* his fecond Brother,
was Gentleman of the Horfe to King
James's Queen, and hath never appeared in any publick Station, nor at Court
fince the *Revolution*; my Lord *Nairn*
comes to Parliament, but never to Court,
and the reft lead a private Life.

This Gentleman is very tall and auk-
ward, fifty Years old.

Marquis of *Annandale*, Prefident of the Council.

IS Chief of the antient Family of *Johnftoun*, and fell in heartily at the *Revolution* with King *William*'s Party, and in a few Months after, entered into a Defign for Reftoring King *James*; which being difcovered by the Apprehenfion of *Nevil Pain*, who was fent from *England* to carry it on, he fubmitted himfelf to King *William*, confeffed his Fault, and had his Pardon.

He was often *out*, and *in* the Miniftry, during the King's Reign; is extremely carried away by his private Intereft; hath good Senfe, with a manly Expreffion, but not much to be trufted; makes as fine a Figure in the Parliament-Houfe, as he does in his Perfon, being tall, lufty, and well fhaped, with a very black Complexion. Her Majefty created him from Earl to Marquis of *Annandale*, and Knight Companion of the *Thiftle*. He is near fifty Years old.

Mar-

Marquis of *Tweedale.*

A Branch of the Antient and Noble Family of *Haye*, Son to that Marquis who was Commiſſioner and Chancellor at the Paſſing of the *Darien*-Company Act ; a great Encourager and Promoter of Trade, and the Welfare of his Country. He hath good Senſe, is very modeſt, much a Man of Honour, and hot when picqued ; is highly eſteemed in his Country, and may make a conſiderable Figure in it now.

He is named by the Queen to be Lord High Chancellor. A ſhort, brown Man, towards ſixty Years old.

Earl

Earl of *Cromarty*, Secretary of State.

WAS Sir *George Mackenzie* of *Torbett*, in the Reign of King *Charles* the Second, and a great oppofer of Duke *Lauderdale*, but fell in with the Duke of *York*, when he was Commiffioner from his Brother King *Charles*.

This Gentleman was made Lord Regifter, and created Vifcount of *Torbett*, and was chief Minifter all the Reft of his Reign, and that of King *James*.

At the *Revolution* he came to Court, and was well recommended to King *William*; but his arbitrary Proceedings had rendered him fo obnoxious to the People, that he could not be employed in that Reign.

On

On the Queen's Acceſſion to the Throne, he was ſent for to Court, and made Secretary of State ; and from Viſcount *Torbett*, created Earl of *Cromarty*.

He is a Gentleman of very polite Learning, and good Parts; hath a great deal of Wit, and is the pleaſanteſt Companion in the World; a great Maſter in *Philoſophy*, and much eſteemed by the Royal Society of *London*. He hath been very handſom in his Perſon ; is tall, fair complexioned, and now paſt ſeventy Years old. *

* This Gentleman was a conſiderable Writer, and his Works are well received by Men of Letters.

Duke

• Duke of *Argyll.*

IS Reprefentative of the Noble Family of *Campbell*; Great-Grandfon to that Earl who was beheaded at the *Reftoration*; Grandfon to that Earl who was beheaded by King *James*; and Son to that Earl who came over with King *William* at the *Revolution*, and by him created Duke.

His Family will not lofe in his Perfon, the great Figure they have made for fo many Ages in that Kingdom ; having all the free Spirit, and good Senfe natural to the Family; being always able to bring Fight Thoufand armed Men into the Field ; and hath the Power of Trying and Executing within his own Territories.

The Queen hath given him the Command of the *Horfe Guards,* which his

his Father alſo had; and made him one of the Knights Companions of the *Thiſtle*. Few of his Years hath a better Underſtanding, nor a more manſy Behaviour. He hath ſeen moſt of the Courts of *Europe*, is very handſom in his Perſon, fair complexioned; about twenty-five Years old.

[illegible], covetous, cunning Scot, has [illegible] principle but his own Interest; [illegible] in his whole Conduct.

Earl

Earl of *Roxburgh*.

IS Reprefentative of the Ancient Family of *Ker*, near the Borders of *England*, and Son to that Earl of *Rox-
burgh* who was going to *Scotland* with
the Duke of *York* in the Reign of King
Charles the Second.

He is a young Gentleman of great
Learning and Virtue ; knows all the
Antient Languages thoroughly, and
fpeaks moft of the Modern, perfectly
well, without Pedantry : Is a fine Gentleman, and lives up to his Quality ;
hath a good Eftate, is comely, in his
Perfon, brown complexioned, about
twenty-five Years old.

Hai

Marquis of *Montrose*.

IS Reprefentative of the Antient and Noble Family of *Graham* ; great Grandfon to that famous *Montrofe*, who was Hanged and Quartered for King *Charles* the Firft ; and Grandfon, by the Mother, to the Duke of *Rothes*.

He inherits all the great Qualities of thofe two Families, with a Sweetnefs of Behaviour, which charms all thofe who know him ; hath improved himfelf in moft Foreign Courts ; is very beautiful in his Perfon, and about twenty-five Years old.

Now very homely, and makes a very sorry appearance.

Duke

Duke of *Gordon.*

[S Grandſon to the Marquis of *Hunt-ley,* who was Beheaded for King *Charles* the Firſt. The Eſtate of the ſamily was then forfeited, and given to ɱy Lord of *Argyll,* and the Family di-ided, with a Deſign of Extirpation ; ɒt on the *Reſtoration* of King *Charles* ɲe Second, the Honour, with the Eſtate, ɰas reſtored to this Gentleman.

He was bred up in the Religion of ɩs Family, who had been always *Roman 'atholicks,* and ſtill ſhewed his Diſlike ɔ the Meaſures of King *James,* for ringing that Religion into *Scotland* gain; eſpecially the taking off the *Penal-aws* and *Teſts.*

He was created a Duke, and Knight-Companion of the *Thiſtle*; and had the Command of *Edenburgh*-Caſtle, which

he

he maintained at the *Revolution* againſt King *William*, till he obtained the Gift made by King Charles, of his Eſtate, confirmed and ratified alſo by King *William*, with a General Pardon for all his Family, and then ſurrendered it; having never received any Order from King *James*, either for *holding* or *giving* it up.

He came to *London*, and made his Submiſſion to King *William*, but not being received as he thought his Service, and the great Power of his Family deſerved, he went privately into *France*, where he was alſo very coldly received, being denied Admittance till he juſtified his Conduct as to the Surrender of *Edenburgh*-Caſtle. He printed *A Journal of that Siege*, in *French*, for the Satiſfaction of that Court; but this did not entirely reconcile him, therefore he left *St. Germains en Laye*, and retired into *Switzerland*, where he was taken Priſoner, ſent into *Holland*, and from thence tranſported into *Scotland*; where he hath

led

ed a very uneafy Life ever fince, being oftner a Prifoner, than at Liberty.

He hath a great many good *Links* in him, but they do not all make a compleat *Chain*.

He is certainly a very fine Gentleman, and underftands Converfation, and the *Belles Lettres* ; is well bred ; made for the Company of Ladies, but is very covetous, which extremely eclipfes him.

The *Priefts*, and *New Converts* in King *James*'s Reign, reprefented him to be a *Libertine* and a *Fop*, becaufe he would not concur in their Meafures for ruling the Kingdom ; but his Character coming from People of his own Profeffion, made it pafs current with thofe who did not know him.

He is a *Roman-Catholic*, becaufe he was bred fo, but otherwife thinks very little of *Revealed Religion*.

He hath a good Eftate, which, notwithftanding his Turns, he improves.

He is very handfom, and taller than the ordinary Size; thin, dreffes well, but is fomewhat finical, refembling the *French*. Paft fifty Years old.

Mar-

Marquis of *Lothian,*

IS Chief of the *Carrs,* a good Family in both Kingdoms; Active in the *Revolution* against King *James.* His Father then being alive, he was made Lord *Jedburg,* and had a Regiment of Dragoons given him, which he kept all the Reign of King *William.* He hath abundance of Fire, and may prove a Man of Business, when he applies himself that Way: Laughs at all *Revealed Religion,* yet sets up for a Pillar of *Presbytery,* and proves the surest *Card* in their *Pack;* being very zealous, though not devout.

He married my Lord *Argyll's* Daughter in King *James's* Reign, when the Father was outlawed, the Estate forfeited, and the Children starving, purely out of a Principle of Honour, believing they suffered wrongfully.

O 3   He

After King *William*, by an Army, had endeavoured with great Expence, to reduce the *Highlands* of *Scotland* in vain, this Gentleman undertook it fingly, with Ten Thoufand Pounds; and effecting it in fuch a Manner, as to get Thanks from King *James* for faving his People whom he could not fuccour. He was rewarded by King *William* for his Service.

He knows neither Honour, nor Religion, but where they are mixed with Intereft, and then they ferve as fpecious Pretences. He plays the *fame Game* with the *Williamites*, as he did with the *Jacobites*; and as the Bifhop of *Munfter* did with *England*, *France*, and *Holland* in the Year 1674, viz. *Always on the fide he can get moft by; and will get all he can of both.*

He is of a fair Complexion, has the Gravity of a *Spaniard*, now paft fixty Years old.   Earl

Earl of *Sutherland,*

[S Chief of one of the antienteſt and moſt Noble Families in *Scotland,* His Father being alive at the *Revolution.* This Gentleman was known by the Name of Lord *Strathnaver,* had a Regiment given him, and followed the King all his Campaigns in *Flanders.*

He is a very honeſt Man, a great Aſſertor of the Liberties of the People; hath a good, rough Senſe; is open and free ; a great lover of his Bottle and his Friend ; brave in his Perſon, which he hath ſhewn in ſeveral Duels; too familiar for his Quality, and often keeps Company below it. Is a fat, fair complexioned Man. Forty-five Years old.

A Blundering, rattle Paſed Drunken Sot.

Earl

Earl of *Melvil*,

IS the Reprefentative of a very Honourable Family in *Scotland* (his Father being alive at the *Revolution*) confpicuous for its Zeal againft *Popery* fince the firft *Reformation*. This Gentleman was much in the Intereft of the Duke of *Monmouth*, and followed his Fortunes.

At the *Revolution* he came over with King *William*, was made Secretary of State for that Kingdom; created from Lord to Earl, and Commiffioner to the firft Parliament. His *eldeft* Son had the Management of the Revenue, and his *fecond* Son, the Earl of *Leven*, was made Governour of *Edenburgh*-Caftle, and had a Regiment; and indeed the Adminiftration of the whole Affairs of *Scotland* were in his Family for fome Years.

On the Queen's Acceffion to the Throne, He and his Son were difmiffed from all their Employments.

He

He hath neither Learning, Wit, nor common Converſation; but a Steadineſs of Principle, and a firm Boldneſs for *Presbyterian Government*, in all Reigns, hath carried him through all theſe great Employments; and his Weakneſs made him the fitter Tool; for my Lord *Portland*, and Mr. *Carſtairs* ſupported him.

He makes a very mean Figure in his Perſon, being low, thin, with a great Head, a long Chin, and little Eyes; is ſeventy Years old.

Secretary *Johnstoun*, now Lord Regiſter.

IS a younger Son of my Lord *Warriſton*, who was beheaded at the *Reſtauration*. On this Misfortune of his Family, this Gentleman was ſent into *Holland*, where he ſtudied the Civil Law, and had the Character of the greateſt Proficient that ever was in *Utrecht*. When he had finiſhed his Studies, he went into *Italy*, where making an Acquaintance with my Lord *Romney*, he was by him inſtructed in the Secrets of the *Revolution*, and employed by that Lord to come privately into *England*, which he did ſuccefsfully.

On King *William*'s Acceſſion to the Throne, he was ſent Envoy to *Berlin*, and from thence recalled and made Secretary of State for *Scotland*.

He

He is the firft who fhewed the Commons of that Kingdom their Strength, and to eftablifh them on a Foot independent on the Nobility (to whom they have always been Slaves) on the fureft way to make their Conftitution lafting, and to make them a flourifhing People. He did great Service alfo in *England*, he difcovered the *La Hogue* Defcent, and had better Intelligence from *France* than any about the King; this gave him great Credit at Court, but created him Enemies and Enviers in both Kingdoms, he was a zealous Promoter of Men of *Revolution* Principles, and a faithful Servant to the Caufe; but paffing a Bill in the Parliament of *Scotland*, for eftablifhing an *African* and *American* Company, which the Parliament of *England* reprefented of ill Confequence to their Trade ; he was at once thrown out of all: and what was very ftrange, the *Whigs*, whofe Intereft it was to fupport him, joined in the

Blow

Blow. This foured him fo, as never to be reconciled all the King's Reign, tho' much efteemed; but now by the *Queen* he is made Lord *Regifter*; the beft Employment in *Scotland*. ·

acheron He is very honeft, yet fomething too *a* credulous and fufpicious; endued with a great deal of Learning and Virtue; is above little Tricks, free from Ceremony; and would not tell a Lye for the World. Very knowing in the Affairs of Foreign Courts, and the Conftitution of both Kingdoms; a tall, fair Man, and towards fifty Years old.

as of the greateſt Knaves even in Scotland.

ames Stuart, Lord Advocate.

WAS a younger Son of the Family of *Colckners* in the *Weft* of cotland, and bred to the Law; in which 'rofeffion he was in good Efteem in the leign of King *Charles* the Second; being fufpected to be one of the Advifers f my Lord *Argyll's* Explanation of the *'eft*, was obliged to retire to *Holland*, nd was declared fugitive; he continued n *Holland* all that Reign; but upon King *James's* fetting up a Difpenfing 'ower, and defigning to pull down the Church by the Diffenters; this Gentleman was thought a fit Tool for the Purpofe, and was fent for by the Court of *England*. He wrote two Letters to *Monfieur Fagel*, when Penfionary of *Holland*, n the King's taking off the *Penal Laws*, vhich with *Monfieur Fagell's* Anfwer, vere afterwards printed. It was fome Time after the *Revolution*, that King
William

William would be reconciled to him, and then made him *Lord Advocate*; in which Poſt the Queen continues him.

He is one of the greateſt Civilians of the Age, or of any Country; of great Natural Parts, yet ſeems plain, affable, and Familiar, and affects want of Ceremony, is of middle Stature, and ſeventy Years old.

Mr.

Mr. *Carstairs,*

[S a *Presbyterian* Minister who fled
from *Scotland*, after the Insurrection
or Religion, in the Reign of King
Charles the Second; was once taken
Prisoner in *England*, and sent down
into *Scotland*, where he underwent the
Torture, and confessed the Designs then
on Foot; he afterwards retired into that
Kingdom, and came over at the *Revoluti-*
on with the Prince of *Orange*; he contrac-
ed in *Holland* an intimate Acquain-
ance with my Lord *Portland*, and was
one of his Family; he was made Chap-
ain to the King, for the Kingdom of
Scotland, had the Revenue of a Bishop-
rick given him for his Salary; he attended the King all his Campaigns, and
was allowed 500 *l.* each Campaign for
his Equipage.

P   As

Earl of *Kijlle*,

IS eldeſt Son to my Lord *Stairs*; ł was Preſident of the Seſſions i the Reign of King *Charles* the Secon and fled to *Holland* after the Duke *York*'s Parliament in that Kingdom.

This Gentleman, notwithſtanding ł Father's Diſgrace, was made *Lord ⅃ vocate* in the Reign of King *Jamı* and at the *Revolution*, his Father coı ing over with King *William*, was reſtoı to his former Employments, of *Prı dent* and *Secretary of State*, with ı Lord *Melvil*, and then with Mr. *Joı ſtoun*, who at laſt threw him out, ı hath he made any tolerable Figure ſin

On the Queen's Acceſſion to Throne, he was from Lord *Stairs* (ated Earl of *Kijlle*. He is a very gı Law'

awyer, of great natural Parts, and
cetious Converſation ; made always a
tter Companion, than a Stateſman,
ing naturally very indolent; is hand-
m in his Perſon, tall, fair, turned of
ty Years old.

Earl

Earl Marifchal,

IS Reprefentative of the Antient and Noble Family of *Keith*, and Hereditary great Marfhal of the Kingdom; he always oppofed the Meafures of King *William*'s Reign, but waited on the Queen, at her Acceffion to the Throne, and acknowledged her Government.

He is very wild, inconftant, and paffionate; does every thing by Starts, hath abundance of flafhy Wit; and by reafon of his Quality, hath good Intereft in the Country ; all Courts endeavour to have him on their Side, for he gives himfelf Liberty of talking, when he is not pleafed with the Government.

He is a *thorough Libertine*, yet fets up mightily for Epifcopacy, a hard Drinker, a thin Body, a middle Stature, ambitious of Popularity, forty-five Years old.

Earl

Earl of *Aberdeen*.

WAS Sir *George Gordon* of *Haddo*, in the Reign of King *Charles* the Second, and a Lord of the Seffions. When the Duke of *York* came to *Scotland* he made him Prefident, and on the Duke of *Rothes*'s Death, he was created a Peer, and *Lord High Chancellor* of the Kingdom; but not proving fo pliable to the Popifh Party as was expected, he was in King *James*'s Reign thrown out again, nor would he ever appear in all the Reign of King *William*, nor does he under the prefent Queen.

He is very knowing in the Laws and Conftitution of his Country, and is believed to be the folideft Statefman in *Scotland*, a fine Orator, fpeaks flow, but ftrong, is towards feventy Years old.

Earl

Earl of *Marchmont*.

WAS Sir *Patrick Home* of *Pol-warth*, a Branch of the Antient Family of *Home*; he was one of those in the designed Insurrection (called *Shaftsbury's Plot*) in King *Charles* the Second's Reign, and not appearing on his Accusation, was declared a Traytor, and his Estate confiscated; he came over from *Holland* with my Lord *Argyll*, in the Duke of *Monmouth's* Expedition, and had the good luck to escape to *Holland* again, and came over at the *Revolution* with the Prince of *Orange*, who created him Lord *Polwarth*; and in some Years after, made him *Lord High Chancellor*, and created him Earl of *Marchmont*; he was also sometime *Lord High Commissioner*.

On the Queen's Accession to the Throne, he was discharged from all his Employments; he hath been a fine Gentleman,

:man, of clear Parts, but always a
over of fet long Speeches, and could
irdly give Advice to a private Friend
ithout them; zealous for the Presby-
rian Government in the Church, and
; *Divine Right*, which was the great
lotive that encouraged him againft the
rown; Bufinefs and Years have now al-
ioft wore him out; he-hath been hand-
m and lovely; and was fo fince King
'*illiam* came to the Throne, towards
venty Years old.

Earl of *Marr*.

IS Reprefentative of one of the Anti-enteft and moft noble Families in *Scotland*, hereditary Guardians of the Kings and Queens of that Kingdom, during their Minority, and hereditary Keeper of *Sterling Caflle*. This Gentleman hath not made any great Figure farther yet, than being of the Privy Council both to King *William* and this Queen.

He is a very good Manager in his private Affairs, which were in Diforder when his Father died, and is a ftaunch Countryman, fair Complexioned, low Stature, and thirty Years old.

is crooked. Esteemed one a Gentleman good sense and good nature.

Earl

Earl of *Dalkeith*.

IS Chief of an Ancient Family in *Scotland*, and eldeſt Son of the late Duke of *Monmouth*, who was Beheaded, 1686.

This Gentleman never appeared much in the Reign of King *William*, being afraid of giving the King any Jealouſy.

Since the Queen came to the Throne, he went to *Scotland*, makes a good Figure, and was created Knight of the *Thiſtle*.

He is a very fair complexioned good Man, not forty Years old.

Andrew

Andrew Fletcher, of *Salton*,

IS a Gentleman of a fair Eſtate in *Scotland*, attended with the Improvement of a good Education. He was Knight of the Shire for *Lothian*, in that Parliament wherein the Duke of *York* was Commiſſioner, in the Reign of King *Charles* the Second; and openly oppoſed the arbitrary Deſigns of that Prince, and the fatal Bill of Acceſſion, which obliged him wiſely to retire firſt to *England*, and then to *Holland*.

The Duke of *York* could not forgive his Behaviour in that Parliament : They ſummoned him to appear at *Edenburgh*, which he not daring to do, he was declared a Traytor, and his Eſtate confiſcated. He retired to *Hungary*, and ſerved ſeveral Campaigns under the Duke of *Lorrain*; returned to *Holland* after the Death of King *Charles* the Second, and

came

came over to *England* with the Duke of
Monmouth ; had the Misfortune to fhoot
the Mayor of *Lime*, after his Landing ;
on which Accident he returned again to
Holland, and came over at the *Revolution*
with the Prince of *Orange*.

He is fo zealous an Affertor of the
Liberties of the People, that he is too
jealous of the growing Power of all
Princes, in whom he thinks Ambition
fo natural, yet he is not for trufting the
beft of Princes with a Power which *ill*
ones may make ufe of againft the People ; believing all Princes are made *by*
and *for* the good of the People ; and
thinks Princes fhould have no Power but
that of *doing Good*. This made him op-
pofe King *Charles*, and King *James*,
and withftand the giving fo much Power
to King *William*, whom he never would
ferve : Nor does he ever come into the
Adminiftration of *this Queen* ; but ftands
up as a ftout Pillar for the Conftitution
in the Parliament of *Scotland*.

He

He is a Gentleman steady in his Principles, of nice Honour, with abundance of Learning ; brave as the Sword he wears, and bold as a Lion. A sure Friend, but an irreconcileable Enemy ; would *lose his Life readily*, to *serve his Country* ; and would not do a *base Thing* to *save it*. His Thoughts are large, as to Religion, and could never be brought within the Bounds of any particular *Sect* ; nor will he be under the Distinction of *Whig* or *Tory* ; saying, these Names are only used to cloak the Knavery of both Parties.

His *Notions* of *Government* are too fine spun, and can hardly be lived up to by Men subject to the common Frailties of Nature ; neither will he give Allowance for extraordinary Emergencies ; witness the Duke of *Shrewsberry*, with whom he had always been very intimate ; yet the Duke being made Secretary of State, a *second Time*, purely to

save

fave his Country, this Gentleman would never be in common Charity with him afterwards : And my Lord *Spenfer*, now Lord *Sunderland*, on Voting for the Army, was ufed by him much after the fame Manner.

He hath written fome excellent Tracts, but not publifhed in his Name ; and hath a very fine Genius ; is a low, thin Man, brown Complexion, full of Fire, with a ftern, four, Look, and fifty Years old. *

* His Works are now publifhed under his Name in one Volume 8vo.

A most arrogant conceited Codak in Politicks, can not endure the leaft contradiction in any of his Visions & Paradoxes.

Mr.

Mr. *Cockburn* of *Ormeston,*

IS the Reprefentative of a very good Family, which was the Firft in *Scotland*, confpicuous for the *Reformation*, in the Reign of *Mary* of *Scotland*, and *Edward* the Sixth of *England*, and hath been a zealous Affertor of *Presbytery* ever fince.

This Gentleman entered heartily into the Meafures of the *Revolution*, and was zealous all King *William's* Reign, efpecially for the *Church-Government of Presbytery*; was made *Lord Juftice Clerk*, and a Privy-Counfellor by King *William*; and fome Time after *Lord Treafurer Deputy*, or *Chancellor of the Exchequer*.

On the Queen's Acceffion to the Throne, he was difmiffed from all his Pofts.

He

He is a *Bigot* to a Fault, and hardly n common Charity with any Man out of the *Verge* of *Presbytery* ; but otherwife a very fine Gentleman in his Perfon and Manners ; juft in his Dealings ; hath good Senfe, of a fanguine Complexion, towards fifty Years old.

Sir

Sir *James Maxwell*, of *Polloc*

WAS in the Reigns of King *Charl* and King *James*, a great Su*p* porter and Entertainer of the profecut*e* *Presbyterian Clergy*, and often fined f*o* fo doing.

At the *Revolution* he was made *Lo* of the *Seffions*, and afterwards *Lord Chi* *Juftice Clerk*, a *Privy Counfellor*, a*r* *Lord of the Treafury*.

On the Queen's Acceffion to t*h* Throne, he was difmiffed from all h Employments.

He is a very honeft Gentleman, no extraordinary Reach, zealous for t*h* *Divine Right of Presbytery*, which hurri him often to do hard Things to M*e*

f less confined Principles, thinking it,
oing God good Service.

He is a very fat, fair Man, towards
ixty Years old.

Earl

Earl of *Marſh*, Governour of *Edenburgh* Caſtle.

IS Brother to the preſent Duke of *Queensberry*.

He was Lieutenant-Colonel of a Regiment of Horſe in King *James's*, and a *Nonjuror* the greateſt Part of King *William's* Reign.

He hath no great Genius, but is a good-natured Gentleman; handſom in his Perſon, turned of fifty Years old.

Earls of *Rothes*, and *Hadingtoun*,

ARE two Brothers ; Grandſons to that Duke of *Rothes*, who made ſo great a Figure in the Reign of King *Charles* the Second, and was Son to the Earl of *Haddingtoun*, who married the Heirs of *Rothes*.

They are both warm Aſſertors of the Liberty of the People, and in great Eſteem in their Country.

My Lord *Rothes* is of vigilant Application for the Service of his Country.

The other hath a Genius whenever he thinks fit to apply himſelf.

Neither of them are thirty Years old.

Earl

Earl of *Lauderdale*,

IS Nephew to that Duke of *Lauder-dale*, who was the great Favourite of King *Charles* the Second.

This Gentleman being a *Younger* Son of a *Younger* Brother, applied himſelf to the Study of the Law, and deſigned in his Profeſſion ; but his *Elder* Brother, my Lord *Maitland* dying in *France*, he came to the Honours, was made a Privy-Counſellor by King *William*, and one of the *Lords of the Seſſions*, and *Exche-quer*.

He is a Gentleman that means well to his Country, but comes far ſhort of his Predeceſſors, who, for three or four Generations, were *Chancellors*, and *Se-cretaries of State* for that Kingdom.

He

He is a well-bred Man, handſom in
is Perſon, fair Complexioned, and to-
rards fifty Years old. *

* It was at the Requeſt of his Uncle, that Dr.
urnet drew up his Solutions of Two *Caſes* of
onſcience concerning *Polygamy* and *Barrenneſs.*
oth omitted in the Hiſtory of *his Own Time.*
ee *Appendix*, Numb. II.

Lord *Blantire*.

IS a Branch of the Antient and Noble
Family of *Stuart*, Dukes of *Lenox*;
and being left a confiderable Eftate by
the late Dutchefs, is like to raife his
Family again.

He is a very bufy Man for the *Liberty* and *Religion* of his Country; yet
whatever Party gets the better, he can
never get into the Adminiftration; he
is very zealous for the *Revolution*, raifed
a Regiment, which King *William* broke
when all was quiet.

When the Queen came to the Throne,
he was fent up as one of the Commiffioners, with an Addrefs for a new Parliament, and made a mighty Stir at
Court; but neither his Endeavours for
the Publick, nor himfelf, fucceeded.

He

He is a little active Man, but thinks only fometimes right; and can neither *fpeak* nor *act*, but by *over-doing* fpoils all.

He loves to be employed, and therefore is often made the *Finder* of a *Party*; can *ftart* the *Hare*, but hath no other Part in the *Chace*; makes but a mean Figure in his Perfon, very low of Stature, fhort fighted, fair Complexioned, towards fifty Years old.

Murray

Murray of *Philliphough*, late Lord *Regiſter*.

IS Repreſentative of an Antient Family, near the Borders of *England*; He was diſcovered in a Deſign of making an Inſurrection in *Scotland* in the Time of *That* which was called the *Shaftesbury-Plot* in *En land*; and to ſave his Life and Eſtate, was an Evidence in that *Kingdom*, as *Howard* of *Eskrick* was in *England*.

He was made *Lord of the Seſſions* at the *Revolution*; and in ſome Time after *Lord Regiſter*, and went out of that Office, along with the Duke of *Queenſ-berry*; he is a Gentleman of clear Natural Parts; and notwithſtanding of that unhappy Step, of being an Evidence to ſave his Life, continued ſtill a great Countryman; of a fair Complexion, fat, middle Stature, turned of fifty Years old.   Earl

Earl of *Glasgow*, Lord Trea-surer Deputy.

IS a Gentleman in the *West* of *Scotland*, of the Name of *Boyle*; was brought to Court by the Duke of *Queensberry*, in the Reign of King *William*, and preferred from a Private Gentleman to be Viscount *Boyle*.

On the Queen's Accession to the Throne, he was made *Lord Treasurer Deputy*, and created Earl of *Glasgow*.

He is a Gentleman of Application and Capacity ; a fat, fair Man, about forty Years old.

Lord

Lord *Belhaven,*

IS a Branch of the Family of *Hamilton,* and was the only Peer who opposed the *Act of Succeſſion* in *Scotland,* when the Duke of *York* was preſent; for which he was ſent Priſoner to the Caſtle of *Edenburgh.*

He hath been angry with the Adminiſtration of all Reigns ſince, becauſe he can never get into any Poſt. Sets up for a Patriot; loves to make long Speeches in Parliament, and hath the Vanity to Print them. A rough, fat, black, noiſy Man, more like a Butcher than a Lord. Turned of fifty Years old.

Earl

Earl of *Home,*

'S the Reprefentative of the Noble Family of that Name.

He is endued with very good Parts; a firm Countryman; but never would knowledge King *William.*

A tall, flovenly Man, paft fixty Years d.

Earl

He is a black Man, of a middle Stature, with a sanguine Complexion; and one of the pleasantest Companions in the World. Towards sixty Years old.

Wm Temple told me he was a very valuable & good Scholar; I once saw him

Earl

Earl of *Perth,*

IS Reprefentative of the Antient and Noble Family of *Drummond.* In his ounger Years he was a zealous *Iresbyterian,* but coming to *England,* to the Court of King *Charles* the Second, he turned to the Church of *England,* and was all that Reign very zealous for *Epifcopacy* ; made Lord Juftice General, and afterwards, Lord High Chancellor.

When King *James* came to the Throne, he declared himfelf a *Roman atholick,* and was a violent carrier on of l the Arbitrary Proceedings in that .eign.

He was taken Prifoner at the *Revotion* ; but, after fome Years, he was t at Liberty, and went to *France,* where he was made Governour to the pretended) Prince of *Wales* ; in which oft he now continues at St. *Germains.*

R   He

He was always violent for the Party he efpoufed, and is paffionately proud; tells a Story very prettily ; is capricious, a thorough Bigot, and hath been *fo* in *each* Relrgion, while he profeffed it.

He is of middle Stature, with a quick Look ; of a brown Complexion, and towards Fifty Years old.

Earl

Earl of *Melfort,*

S Brother to the Earl of *Perth*, and
was *Deputy-Governor* to the Caſtle
Edenburgh, when the Duke of *York* and
s Dutcheſs came to *Scotland*. Being
ery handſom, and a fine Dancer, he got
far into her Royal Highneſs's Favour,
to be made Lord *Treaſurer-Deputy* ; and
1 their Highneſſes arrival at *London*, he
as ſent for to Court, and made *Secre-*
ry of State, ; in which Poſt he conti-
ed all the Reign of King *James*, was
eated Earl of *Melfort*, made Knight-
ompanion of the *Thiſtle*, and was one
: the chief Favourites of the Court.

He followed King *James* into *France*
1d *Ireland*, was there made Knight of
ie *Garter*, and ſent Ambaſſador to *Rome*.
le afterwards had the chief Admini-
ration of St. *Germains* for ſome Years,
ll a Letter he had wrote from *Paris*

to St. *Germains*, which was, by Miſtake, put into the Poſt for *England*, (and printed there) ſo much incenſed the *French* King againſt him, as to baniſh him to *Angers*, where he ſtill continues.

He is very ambitious, hath abundance of lively Senſe, will ſt.ck at nothing to gain his End ; a well bred Gentleman, underſtands the *Belles Lettres* ; is very proud ; cannot bear a Rival in Buſineſs ; nor is he much to be truſted himſelf, but where his Ambition can be fed.

He is tall, black, ſtoops in the Shoulders, thin, and turned of fifty Years old.

Earl

Earl of *Belcarras*,

WAS efteemed a very good Countryman in the Reign of King *Charles* the Second; yet brought in by the two Brothers, *Perth* and *Melfort*, in the Reign of King *James*, to be their Affiftants, in carrying on the Arbitrary Meafures of that Reign : But he fo incenfed the People by his Proceedings, that he was neceffitated to fly at the *Revolution*.

He then went to *France*, but not meeting with the Encouragement he expected, retired to *Hamburgh*, and is not yet reconciled to his Country.

He is a Gentleman of very good natural Parts, hath abundance of Application; handfom in his Perfon, very fair ; and towards fixty Years old.

Earl

Earl of *Strathmore*,

IS Reprefentative of the Family of *Lyon*. The firft of the Name, by marrying a Daughter of a King of *Scotland*, was made a Lord. They have fince made a Figure in the Kingdom, and have been Chancellors by the Title of Lord *Glomes*.

This Gentleman is well bred, and good-natured; hath not yet endeavoured to get into the *Adminiftration*, being no Friend to *Presbytery*.

He hath two of the fineft Seats in *Scotland*, viz. *Glomes*, and *Caftle-Lyon*; is tall, fair, and towards fifty Years old.

Earl

Earl of *Arrol*,

IS Reprefentative of the Antient and Noble Family of *Haye*, and Hereditary High Conftable of *Scotland*.

The prefent Earl hath lived retired fince the *Revolution*. He is of a brown Complexion, middle Stature, towards feventy Years old.

His Son, my Lord *Haye*, is one of the hopefulleft young Gentlemen in the Kingdom ; and an Enemy to *Presbytery*, not twenty-five Years old.

Earl

Earl of *Morton*,

IS one of the Antient Family of *Douglas*.

This Gentleman was zealous for the *Revolution*, and always a Follower of the Duke of *Queensberry* ; of no great Capacity, but for the Ladies ; and hath been famous that Way.

He is very fair, fanguine complexion-ed, well fhaped, taller than the ordinary Size, and fifty-five Years old.

Earl

Earl of *Crawford*,

IS Reprefentative of the Antient and Noble Family of *Lindfey*, who have been often very confpicuous in their Country.

This Gentleman's Grandfather was Lord High Treafurer in the Reign of King *Charles* the Second; and his Father was the zealoufeft Man in the World for the *Revolution*; was Prefident to feveral Parliaments of King *William*, and Prefident of the Council and Treafury; but, he hath neither *Genius*, nor *Gufto* for Bufinefs.

King *William* gave him a Regiment of Foot, and afterwards made him a Lieutenant-Colonel of the Horfe-Guards.

Earl

Earl of *Weems*,

IS Reprefentative of the Antient Family of that Name, and is a very fine Gentleman.

He, as his Family hath ever been, is zealous for the Liberty of the People, and for bringing down the Power of the *Crown*.

He hath not yet been in the Adminiftration ; is a fine Perfonage, and very beautiful ; hath good Senfe, and is a Man of Honour. About thirty Years old.

Earl of *Murray,*

IS of the Royal Family of STUART, lineally defcended from the firft Earl, natural Son to King *James* the Fifth of *Scotland,* who was Regent during the Misfortunes of his Sifter *Mary,* and the firft Eftablifher of the *Proteftant Religion* in *Scotland.* This Gentleman was one of the firft Secretaries of that Kingdom, in the Reign of King *Charles* the Second, and continued in this Poft by King *James,* was fent down Commiffioner to take off the *Penal-Laws,* which his great Anceftor laid on, but did not fucceed therein; he turned *Roman Catholick,* was made *Knight Companion* of the *Thiftle,* and at the *Revolution,* retired to his Country Seat at *Durmberfle,* where he leads a quiet Life, without even thinking of returning to the Adminiftration.

He is a very good natured Man, and was wrought upon by the Court to do whatever they pleafed; he is very fat and fair, near feventy Years old.

N. B. The *Popiſh Families* in *Scotland*; beſides thoſe which I have already mentioned, in the foregoing *Characters*, are as follow, *viz.*

I. *Maxwell*, Earl of *Nitheſdale*.

II. *Stuart*, Earl of *Traquair*.

III. *Mackenzie*, Earl of *Seaforth*.

IV. *Semple*, Lord *Semple*.

V. A Branch of *Macdonalds* in the *Highlands*.

VI. The Clan of *Mackleans* in the *Weſtern Iſlands*.

AN

AN
APPENDIX
OF
Original PAPERS.

APPENDIX.

NUMBER I.

In the Name of God, Amen. I GILBERT BURNET, Doctor in Divinity, and Bishop of *Salisbury*, being in good ealth, and perfect and found in my Mind, make and ordain my Last Will and Tesnent, in Manner and Form following: at is to say, First, I commend my Soul to Good and Gracious God, who has blessed in the Course of my Life with great and nal Blessings, both Spiritual and Temporal, d before whom I have endeavoured to lk with great Integrity and Simplicity of art, and have exercised my self to have

A   always

always a Confcience void of Offence towards
my God, and towards all Men, both in the
private Capacity of a Chriftian, and in the
Difcharge of the Publick Trufts and Stations
to which he has called me, though with many
Failings, and great Infirmities, for which I
humbly defire (and truft to obtain) Mercy
and Pardon by the Merits and Interceffion
of *Jefus Chrift*, my bleffed Saviour and
Redeemer, in whom alone I put my Truft,
and by whom I fly to the Mercies of God,
hoping he will accept of my fincere Repen-
tance, and forgive all my Sins, and that he
will affift me with his Spirit, and guide
me through the Valley of the Shadow of
Death, and receive me into his Kingdom and
Glory.

I live and die a fincere Chriftian, believing
the Truth of that Gofpel which for many
Years I have preached to others. I am a true
Proteftant according to the *Church of England*;
full of Affection and Brotherly Love to all
who have received the *Reformed Religion*, tho'
in fome Points *Different* from our Conftitution.

I die, as I all along lived and profeffed
my felf to be, full of Charity and Tendernefs
for *thofe* among *Us* who yet *Diffent from us*,
and heartily pray that God would heal our
Breaches, and make us like-minded in all
Things,

Things, that fo we might unite our Zeal, and join our Endeavours againſt *Atheiſm* and *Infidelity*, that have prevailed much; and againſt *Popery*, the greateſt Enemy to our *Church*, more to be dreaded than all other Parties whatſoever.

I Will, that my Body be decently but privately buried, in caſe I die at *Salisbury*, in the *South* Ile of the Cathedral, where two of my Children lie buried : And in caſe I die in any other Place, in the Church, or Church-yard of the Pariſh where I may happen to die.*

As to all my Goods, Eſtate, or Furniture of my two Houſes, I order the whole to be appraiſed and ſold, and that my LIBRARY be alſo ſold by Auction, excepting only ſuch Things as I have divided amongſt my Children by a Codicil added to this my Will; and that after my Debts are paid, and my Funeral Charges, and the Legacies hereafter mention-

---

* *His Lordſhip died at his Houſe in St.* John's *Square, in the Pariſh of St.* James Clerkenwell ; *and on* Tueſday March 22. 1714-15, *his Body was interred in that Church, near the Communion-Table, the Pall being ſupported by, his worthy Succeſſor, Dr.* Talbot, *Biſhop of* Oxford, *Dr.* Wake, *Biſhop of* Lincoln, *Dr.* Trimnell, *Biſhop of* Norwich, *Dr.* Evans, *Biſhop of* Litchfield *and* Coventry, *Dr.* Hough, *Biſhop of* Bangor, *and Dr.* Fleetwood, *Biſhop of* Ely.

ed

ed are paid and satisfied, that the whole Produce of all that belongs to me at the Time of
my Decease, shall be divided into Six equal
Parts, of which I give two to my eldest Son
WILLIAM; and one, to every one of the rest of
my Sons and Daughters; with this one Re-
servation, That in Case I do not in my own
Life-time raise *Two Thousand Two Hundred
Twenty* and *Two Pounds, Four Shillings* and
Six Pence, for Two Endowments set forth in
a Codicil added to this my Will, then the Sum
of *Ninety* and *Nine Pounds*, due to me in the
Exchequer, shall be set aside for raising the
said Sum, together with the yearly Interest ari-
sing out of the said *Ninety Nine Pounds*, and
shall be kept apart for the said Endowments,
together with *Fifty Pounds* more, which I give
to my Nephew GILBERT BURNET, Advocate
in *Edenborough*, for the Charge and Trouble
of settling them, according to the Schedule
that I add as a Codicil to this my Will. And
I recommend the Management of this *Ninety
Nine Pounds*, together with the Interest that
will grow out of it, to my worthy Friend,
JOHN WARNER, Goldsmith; and for his Pains
in this, I leave *Fifty Pounds* to his Eldest Son,
my Godson.

Item, I give and devise all the Furniture of
the Great Upper Room in the Palace at *Salisbury*, and of the Chappel there, to my Suc-
cessor

ceffor the Bifhop of *Salisbury*, in the fame manner that my Predeceffor Bifhop WARD left the Furniture in the Parlour of the faid **Palace**.

I appoint all my Servants to be kept toge-ther for a Month after my Deccafe, and to be entertained, or have Board Wages given them ; and I give to every one of them Half a Year's Wages, befides the Wages of the Quarter in which I die.

I give alfo half a Year's Salary to the Ma-fter of my *Charity-School* in *Salisbury*, befides that due for the Salary of the Quarter in which I die.

Item, I appoint *Twenty Pounds* to be divid-ed among the Poor of *Salisbury*, *Five Pounds* to the Poor of the *Clofe*, to be diftributed by Mr HOADLY, and *Five Pounds* to the Poor in the Three Parifhes in the City of *Salisbury*, to be diftributed among them by the Minifters of the three Parifhes at their Difcretion.

Item, I make and conftitute my eldeft Son WILLIAM BURNET, the Executor of this my laft Will and Teftament. In Witnefs where-of, I have hereunto fet my Hand and Seal, on the Twenty-fourth Day of *October* in the Tenth Year of the Reign of our Soveraign

Lady

Lady Queen ANNE, *Anno Domini* One Thouſand ſeven hundred and Eleven.

Gi. Sarum.

Signed, Sealed, and Publiſhed, as the laſt Will and Teſtament of the ſaid Gilbert, *Biſhop of* Salisbury, *in the Preſence of*

John Macknay,
Alexander Le Fort,
John Barnes.

This I add, as a Codicil, *to my Will.*

I Give all my Papers to my Son GILBERT, with this expreſs Order, That none of them be printed; but that he keep them all for his own Uſe, or deſtroy them, as he thinks fit.

     I do only except out of this General Order, a Book intituled, *E S S A Y S and M E D I-*

T A T I O N S

ATIONS on MORALITY *and* RELIGION·
1d the *HISTORY of my own* TIME, tother with the Conclufion, and the *HIS
ORY of my own* LIFE. There are two
ɔpies of this *Hiftory*, one in my own Hand,
d another in the Hand of a Servant. In
e Reading thefe over, I have made feveral
nendments, Deletions. and Additions, hav
ɡ read over fometimes the one Copy, and
netimes the other; fo I order the two Coes to be compared together, that fo all the
terations that I have made may be taken inthe printed Edition. I leave it to the Dif
ɛtion of my Executor, to print the *Book of
SSAYS*, when he pleafes, and limit him
no Time. But for the *HISTORY*, I lit him in the printing of it to fix Years after
ɲ Death, and that it may not be printed
ɔner; but as to the printing it after fix Years,
delaying it longer, I refer that to fuch Di
ɬions as I may give him by Word of Mouth;
ly I require him to print it faithfully as I
ve it, without adding, fuppreffing, or aling it, in any Particular; for this is my pove Charge and Command.

As for any Advantage that may be made by
: Sale of the Copies of thefe Books, or the
ling out my Property in any of my other
oks, I order it to be divided into fix Parts,
which my Eldeft Son WILLIAM, my Exe
A 4 cutor,

cutor, shall have two, and every one of my other Children shall have one.

Gi. Sarum.

Signed, Sealed, and Published, as a Codicil added to my Will, in the Presence of

John Macknay,
Alexander le Fort,
John Barnes.

This I add, as another Codicil, *to my Will.*

WHereas by my Will I have settled a Method for raising *Two* and *Twenty Hundred* and *Two and Twenty Pounds Three Shillings and Six Pence*, which is in *Scottish* Money *Forty Thousand Marks*, it is my Will and Pleasure, that when the said Sum is raised in the Method that I have prescribed, an Account of it shall be sent to my Nephew, Mr. GILBERT BURNET, Advocate, that he may transact for a Legal and secure Way of settling the One Half of the said Sum in, or near, the Parish of *Salton*, upon an Infeofment of Annual Rent, for the due Payment of a *Thousand Marks* yearly, at the Feast and Term of *Martimasse* ; and

of

of fettling the other Half of the faid Sum in
like manner, in, or near, the *Town* and College
of *New Aberdeen*, with fuch Forfeitures, in
cafe of not paying the yearly Sums of a *Thoufand Marks* to the Parifh of *Salton*, and the
College of *New Aberdeen*, as according to the
Laws of *Scotland* can be made; and for his
Trouble and Expence in doing this, I leave
him *Fifty Pounds*.   All this is provided in cafe
that I do not in my own Life-time accomplifh
my Defign in fettling thefe two Endowments.
In *Salton* I order the *Thoufand Marks* to be thus
difpofed of; Thirty Children of the poorer
fort fhall be put to School, to learn Reading,
Writing, and cafting Accompts; to every one
of thefe *Ten Marks Scottifh* fhall be given, to
cloath them in plain Gray Cloaths, all of one
fort; this is *Three Hundred Marks*. After
they have been four Years at School, and are
fit to be bound out to Trades, or to follow
Husbandry, they fhall receive forty *Marks*
a-piece, which is *Four Hundred Marks* more:
But this *Four Hundred Marks*, during thefe
four Years that they are at School, fhall be applied to the building a good *School houfe* near
the Church-yard, and for purchafing half an
Acre of Ground for a Garden and Outlet to the
School-houfe.   I appoint a hundred *Marks* a
Year of Addition to the School-Mafter's Allowance; and *Fifty Marks* a Year to the Increafe of the Library began for the Minifter's
Houfe

House and Use, of which he shall every Three
Years give an Account to the *Lairds* of *Salton*
and *Hermiston*, and to any two neighbouring
Ministers, which they shall be obliged to sign
for his Discharge, unless they can shew Rea-
son to the contrary. The Boys and Girls either to be put to School, or afterwards to
'Prentice, shall be named thus; Twenty by
the *Laird* of *Salton*, and Ten by the Minister,
who shall be chosen out of the other Estates
in the Parish; as also by Turns, Seven of
those to be put to 'Prentice by the *Lairds* of
Salton, and Three by the Minister; and the
next Year Six only by the *Lairds* of *Salton*,
and Four by the Minister. The remaining
Hundred and *Fifty Marks* to be distributed
yearly to the Poor of the Parish by the Minister, with the Approbation of the *Lairds* of
Salton and *Hermiston*, and such others as join
with him in taking care of the Poor of that
Parish. And this Course I order to be continued for ever, as an Expression of my kind
Gratitude to that Parish, who had the first
Fruits of my Labours, and among whom I had
all possible Kindness and Encouragement. I
leave my said Nephew the Visitor and Overseer of this Endowment, that it be carried on
according to my Design, with a Power to him
at his Death to name another Overseer, and
this to continue in a perpetual Succession:
And if any Overseer fails to name another,
then

I refer it to the *Senators* of the *College* of
lice, to infpect and overfee it; with this
refs Provifo, That if any of the faid Over-
s are put to any Charge to have my Will
his Endowment to be faithfully obferved,
hall be reimburfed out of the faid Rent-
:rge of a *Thoufand Marks*, which fhall be
on fuch Branches of it as fhall be thought
the faid Overfeer, together with the Mini-
, and the *Laird* of *Salton*, moft agreeable
ny Intentions in this Endowment. As for
Thoufand Marks which I gave for ever to
College of *New Aberdeen*, in Remem-
nce of my Education there, I order the
rd of *Leyes*, as long as that Eftate is in the
nily of the BURNETS, to name every Year a
olar for the firft Clafs of that College, to
om a *Hundred* and *Fifty Marks* a Year fhall
paid for the four Years Stay in the *College*,
l *Two Hundred Marks* for the two Years after
t, he continuing in the Study of Divinity;
l the next to be nominated a Scholar fhall
re the faid *Hundred* and *Fifty Marks* only
ing the four Years of his being at the *Col-*
·; but the third, who fhall be nominated
be·a Scholar, fhall have the former Provi-
i for the two Years of Divinity which the
rth fhall not have; thus when all are full,
'houfand Marks a Year will anfwer for fou
iolars, and two Students of Divinity. But
ie thefe are to be gradually filled, I appoint
the

the Overplus of the *Thousand Marks* for every Year, till the whole Number is filled up, which will amount to *Two Thousand Seven Hundred Marks*, to be applied to the raising a Building of six Chambers, for the Conveniency of the Scholars. All this I recommend to the *Lairds* of *Leyes*, to execute this with the Consent of the Principal of the said *College*, and the Provost of the said *Town*. The Principal and Regents shall have the Examination of the Scholars so nominated, with a Power to refuse them, so that only fit Persons may enjoy the Benefit of this Endowment. And if any *Laird* of *Leyes* shall take any Reward for any such Nomination, or detain any Part of the Provision made for such Scholars, then the said Nomination shall be for ever lodged with the Provost and Bailies of *New Aberdeen*, for one Turn, and the Principal and Regents of the *College* for the next Turn; which I appoint also shall take Place, in case the *Lairdship* of *Leyes* shall go out of the Name and Family of BURNET: As I do also desire, that to the said Scholarships One of the Name of BURNET may be preferred, if he is duly qualified for it. This I sign and join with my Will.

Gi. Sarum.

Signed, Seal·d, and Publ shed, as a Codicil added to my Will, in the Presence of,

John Macknay,
Alexander Le Fort,
John Barnes.

Whereas

WHereas I, by my laſt Will and Teſtament, ordered all my Eſtate, Arrears
of Rents, Debts and Goods, belonging to me
at the Time of my Death, to be divided into
Six equal Shares, of which Two were provided for my Eldeſt Son WILLIAM, and one
for every one of my other four Children.
—And now upon the Marriage of my Eldeſt
Son †, I have made over to him the ſeveral
Branches mentioned in a Deed bearing Date
the Third Day of *June*, in the Year One
Thouſand, Seven Hundred and Twelve, which
I value at *Three Thouſand Pounds*, I do therefore revoke that Part of my Will, by which
two Shares, out of Six, of my whole Eſtate
are given to him, and appoint, that till a Sum
of *Five Thouſand* and *Seven Hundred Pounds* is
raiſed, and given among my other Children,
Fifteen Hundred Pounds a-piece to Three of
them, and *Twelve Hundred Pounds* to my young-
eſt Son THOMAS, beſides the *Three Hundred
Pounds* that I paid for his Chambers in the *Middle
Temple*, the ſaid WILLIAM ſhall have no other
Title or Right deſcending from me to him :
But when the ſaid Sum of *Five Thouſand* and

* *He married the Daughter of Dr.* Stanhope, *Dean of* Canterbury.

Seven

Seven Hundred Pounds is thus set off for my younger Children, then I confirm my Will with Relation to any Overplus that may belong to me at the Time of my Death, so that it shall be divided into Six equal Shares, of which two shall belong to my said Eldest Son, and one to the other four Children, Share and Share alike. And this I add as a Codicil, and Part of my said last Will and Testament.

Gi. Sarum.

Signed, Sealed, and Published, as a Codicil, and Part of my Will, the fourth Day of June, *One Thousand Seven Hundred and Twelve, in the Presence of*

John Macknay,
Alexander Le Fort,
John Barnes.

WHereas by my last Will and Testament, and by a Codicil added to it, I provided that a Sixth Part of all I shall be possessed of at my Death, shall belong to my Second Daughter, ELIZABETH: And that I have now given her *Fifteen Hundred Pounds*, at her

ᵉr Marriage *. I do now add this as another
Codicil, that till *Fifteen Hundred Pounds* is
given off to my Daughter MARY, and as much
to my Son GILBERT, and *Twelve Hundred* to
my Son THOMAS, she shall demand no Share
of my Goods, by Virtue of that Clause in my
Will; but that when it is done, she shall then
have a Sixth Part of all the Overplus of what
I shall leave at my Death. And this I add as
a Codicil, and as a Part of my said last Will
and Testament.

Gi. Sarum.

Signed, Sealed, and Published, as a
Codicil, *and Part of my Will, the*
Seventeenth Day of April, *One*
Thousand, Seven Hundred and
Fourteen.

John Macknay,
John Barnes,
Joseph Band.

---

* *She married* Richard West, *Esq; late Lord Chancel-*
or of Ireland.

A

A SCHEDULE, *containing the Diſtribution of my Goods among my Children.*

To my Eldeſt Son, WILLIAM.

I Give the Bed, Chairs, Tapeſtry, and the Furniture of the beſt Bed-Chamber in St. *John's*.

I give the Plate that came from *Hanover*.

The Clock in the Parlour at *Salisbury*.

A Pair of Silver Candleſticks, with Snuffers and Snuff-Diſh, at his Choice.

A Gilt Salver, with St. *George's* little Salver.

All the Pictures in the Dining-Room and Parlour at *Salisbury*.

All my Works, bound in Red *Turkey* Leather.

My Mathematical Inſtruments, Wind-pump, and Glaſſes.

The Black Velvet Bed, with the Furniture of that Room.

My Picture by Sir GODFREY KNELLER, after Mr. JOHNSTOUN's Life.

Twelve

Twelve Spoons, ten Forks, two Salts, and the Set of Casters.

Twelve Silver Hafted Knives, with my Crest on them.

The Cabinet in the Great Drawing Room at *Salisbury*.

The *Magna Charta*.

Four Pair of *Holland* Sheets, three Dozen of *Damask* Napkins, with the Appurtenances.

Three Dozen of Diaper Napkins.

Three Pair of Sheets for Servants.

To my Second Son, GILBERT.

I Give all the rest of my Gilt Plate ; and my Repeating Watch.

Gold Medals, to the Value of Fifty Pounds Three Shillings.

All the Pictures in the Dining Room at St. *John's*.

The Furniture of the Room I lie in, at *Salisbury*, together with the Furniture of the Room in which WILLIAM lies.

The Clock in the Room before my Study, at *Salisbury*.

The Picture of the Supper in the Parlour, at St. *John's*.

B   My

My Picture in the Room where my Son WILLIAM lies, at St. *John's*.

A Pair of Silver Candlesticks, with Snuffers and Snuff-Dish ; eight Spoons, eight Forks, a Salt, and a Decanter.

The Tapestry in the Room, without the *King's Room, Salisbury.*

A great Salver, and a small Salver.

The Half of my Silver Medals.

Six Silver Hafted Knives.

BUCK's Bible.

The Polyglot Bible, and Lexicon.

The Great Book of Maps.

All the Furniture, except the Books and Pictures, in my Study at St. *John's*.

Four Pair of *Holland* Sheets.

Three Pair for Servants.

Three Dozen of Damask Napkins, and three Dozen of Diaper, with the Appurtenances, and Three Pair of Sheets for Servants.

To my Eldest Daughter, MARY.

I Give all the Furniture of the *Red Room,* with every Thing in it.

All the Furniture of the Room they now lie in at *Salisbury.*

The Pictures of the Family, done by Mrs. HOADLY.

The Pictures of the Daughter fuckling her Father, in the Parlour at St. *John's.*

The Repeating Table-Clock tipped with Silver.

The Cafe with the twelve fmall Forks, Knives and Spoons.

Six Spoons, fix Forks, and a Salt.

A great Salver, and a fmall one.

The Picture of WILLIAM Duke of *Hamil-on,* in a Gold Cafe.

Two Silver Candlefticks, with Snuffers ind Snuff-Difh.

The Cabinet in my Son's Room at *Salif-bury.*

The Black Silvered Leather, that is with-ut the *Red Room.*

Gold Medals to the Value of Fifty Pounds nd One Shilling.

The Great Bible that lies before me in 1y Chapel.

The Half of all my China Difhes.

This I add as a Codicil to my Will.

Gi. Sarum.

Signed, Sealed, and Published, as a
Codicil added to my Will, in the
Presence of

John Macknay,
Alexander Le Fort,
John Barnes.

In

In *St. James's* Church, *Clerkenwell*, is a fair Marble Monument, fixed to the *East* Wall (*Northward* of the Communion-Table) The *Pediment*, which is Circular, is supported by *Pillasters* of a *Composite* Order, on the Extremities of which, are Urns, and in the *Center* are the Arms of the *See*, and *Burnet*, Impaled in a Shield; on the Freeze are cut in *Relievo*, several Books and Rolls; amongst which is one entitled, H I S T: R E F O R M. And on the *Tablet* underneath is this Inscription:

H. S. E.

GILBERTUS BURNET. S. T. P.

Epifcopus *Sarisburienfis*
Et Nobiliffimi Ordinis à Perifcelide CANCELLARIUS
Natus *Edinburgi*, 18 Die *Septembris.* Anno Dom. 1643.
Parentibus ROBERTO BURNET, Domino de Cremont
ex antiquiffima domo de *Leyes* & RACHELE JOHNSTON
Sorore Domini de *Warifoun*
Aberdonia Literis inftructus Saltoni curæ animarum invigilavit,
Inde Juvenis adhuc S. Stæ. Theologiæ Profeffor in
Academia *Glafgoenfi* electus eft.

Poftquam in *Angliam* tranfiit rem facram per aliquot
Annos in Templo Rotulorum *Londini* adminiftravit, donec
nimis acriter (ut iis qui rerum tum potiebantur vifum eft)
Ecclefiæ Romanæ malas Artes infectatus, ab officio fubmotus eft.
E patria, temporum iniquitate profugus, EUROPAM peragravit.
Et deinceps cum Principe AURIACO reverfus, primus omnium
a Rege GULIELMO & Regina MARIA Præful defignatus
& in fummum tandem fiduciæ teftimonium ab eodem
Principe Duci GLOCESTRIENSI Præceptor dictus eft.

Tyrannidi & Superftitioni femper infenfum fcripta eruditiffima
Demonftrant, nec non Libertatis Patriæ veræque Religionis
ftrenuum femperque indefeffum Propugnatorem. Quarum
utrifque confervandæ fpem unam jam à longo tempore in
Illuftriffima Domo BRUNSVICENSI collocarat. Poftquam
autem Dei Providentia fingulari Regem GEORGIUM
Sceptro BRITANNO potitum confpexerat, brevi jam,
Annorum & felicitatis fatur è vivis exceffit
duxit Uxorem Dominam MARGARITAM KENNEDY Comitis
Caffiliæ filiam, dein MARIAM SCOT *Hagæ* Comitis quæ ei
feptem liberos peperit, quorum adhuc in vivis funt
GULIELMUS, GILBERTUS, MARIA, ELIZABETHA & THOMAS.
Poftremo Uxorem duxit viduam ELIZABETHAM BERKELEY
qua duos liberos fufcepit, fato præmaturo non multo poft extinctos
Ampliffimam pecuniam in pauperibus alendis & in fumptibus, fed
Utilitatem publicam fpectantibus, vivus continuo erogavit, moriens
Duo millia Aureorum ABERDONIÆ SALTONOQUE ad Juventutem pauperiorem
inftituendam Teftamento legavit
Obiit 17 Die Martii, Anno Domini 1714-15. Ætatis 71º.

NUM-

Number II.

BISHOP Burnet in the *History of his Own Time, Folio,* Pag. 261. mentions a *Design, which was set on Foot to Divorce King* CHARLES *from* Queen CATHARINE. On this Occasion (says he) " *Other Stories were* " *given out of the* Queen's *Person, which were* " *false; for I saw a Letter under the King's* " *own Hand, that the Marriage was Consum-* " *mated; others talked of* POLYGAMY; *Lord* " *Lauderdale, and Sir* Robert Murray, *asked* " *my Opinion of these Things; I said, I knew* " *speculative People could say a great deal, in* " *the Way of Argument, for* POLYGAMY *and* " DIVORCE : *Yet those Things were so decried,* " *that they were rejected by all Christian Socie-* " *ties."* However Dr. *Burnet* freely declared his Sentiments on these two Points. He had taken the Pains, to write *two* Arguments in Defence of both. First, Of *Divorce,* in case of *Barrenness.* And of *Polygamy* in general, without any such Motive. These Papers he put into the Hands of Lord *Lauderdale,* and others, with an Intent to farther the Design of Divorcing his Majesty, and thereby of providing, by a *Re-marriage,* Heirs to the Crown,

and

and excluding the Duke of *York.* Why thefe
very curious *Anecdotes* are denied a Place in
our Prelate's remarkable Hiftory, I cannot
affign the Caufe; but this I know, that he
himfelf had inferted them. The late Mr.
Archdeacon *Echard* affuring me, that he had
read them in his Lordfhip's *Manufcript*; and,
as I have obtained exact Copies of them, I
think my felf obliged both in Juftice to the
Bifhop's Memory, as well as the Republick of
Letters, to preferve them for the Information
and Benefit not only of the prefent, but of all
fucceeding Times.

This noble Precedent of *juft* and *Free-Think-
ing,* fhews the Integrity of the Writer, as the
Arguments themfelves do, the honeft Ortho-
doxy of the Divine, in faïrly oppofing the
whole Torrent of Antiquity, the Decrees of
the Church, and the unanimous Opinion of
Civilians, Canonifts, Cafuifts, and Divines in
all Ages.

Thefe Papers were entitled, *Dr.* GILBERT
BURNET'S *Refolution of two important Cafes of
Confcience.* QUESTION the FIRST, *viz.*

Is *a Woman's Barrennefs a juft Ground for
a* DIVORCE, *or for* POLYGAMY?

QUESTION the SECOND. *Is* POLYGAMY *in
any Cafe lawful under the Gofpel.*

The

The Reader is defired to take notice, That the following Copies of thefe two *Refoluti-ons*, are attefted by the learned Dr. *Paterfon*, Archbifhop of *Glafgow*; and the Originals are now in the Cuftody of the Honourable *Archibald Campbell*, Efq; where they may be feen, if any Occafion fhould make it requi-fite to produce them.

The Archbifhop of *Glafgow*'s Attettation is in *this* Form, under his Hand, and Epifco-pal Seal Manual, *viz.*

At *Edenborough*, this fifth Day of *January*, One Thoufand Seven Hundred and Three Years. That the above-written Refolution of thefe two Cafes, *viz.* (is a Woman's Barren-nefs, a juft Ground for Divorce, or Polygamy; and is Polygamy in any Cafe lawful under the Gofpel ?) contained in this and the Two fore-going Pages, is a true Copy of what I faw, read, and copied, from the Original Manufcript, written with Dr. GILBERT BURNET'S own Hand; and which I copied over at *Ham*, in the Year 1680 *; the Original being then in the Poffeffion of the Duke of *Lauderdale*, by whofe Allowance and Confent I took a Co-py of it, I do hereby folemnly attett, as Wit-nefs my Hand and Seal, Day, Year, and Place above-written.   J. GLASGOW, *L. S.*

* *Ham* is a fmall, but very pleafant Village in the County of *Surrey*; where the Duke of *Lauderdale* had a fine Seat.

CASE

CASE *the* FIRST, *Resolved.*

QUÆRITUR *primo;* Is a Woman's *Barrenness* a juft Ground for *Divorce,* or for *Polygamy?* —*Resol.* — For Anfwer muft be better ftated, and Barrennefs declared to be PASSIVE IMPOTENCY or INABILITY; or if a Woman can only *Receive* a Man, that makes her fit only for *Venery,* which is a fecondary End of Marriage, that follows the Fall and Corruption of Mankind; whereas the Primary Intendment of Marriage, which was Antecedent to Man's Sin, is *Propagation:* Whofoever therefore is *incapable* of that, muft be *incapable* of *Marriage;* for as nothing that only tickles the Tafte, but is of fuch a Nature, that it cannot be concoɗed in the Stomach, can be efteemed Meat, fo neither hath he a vital Appetite, who only feels a Relifh in his Mouth when his Stomach can raife no Fermentation in what he fwallows down; fo alfo, if either a Man's *Seed* be incapable of *Fermentation,* or a Woman's *Matrix* be unable to *Ferment,* either of thefe will ftate a Perfon *Impotent.* If therefore it be apparent that a Woman, either through the Situation and Difpofition of her *Parts,* or fome other Quality inherent in

her

her *Matrix*, cannot *Conceive*; this being attested by Phyficians, fhe is to be declared *Barren*. Only from this Cafe fuch Women are to be excepted as are married, after the Age of Forty or Forty-five Years, in whom the natural *Fœcundity* may be fuppofed to be dried up; and in that Cafe a Man doth himfelf the Injury by fuch a voluntary Choice, and there is no Reafon he fhould be inabled to undo it. A great Difference is alfo to be made betwixt a *natural Barrennefs*, and that which is meerly *Cafual*. A Woman being then found *naturally Barren*, nothing of *Divorce* or *Polygamy* is to be confidered, but fne is to be declared *incapable* of *Marriage*, as in the Cafe of *Frigidity* on the Man's Part: And fo the *Marriage* is to be annulled. This is a fhorter and a more expedite Way than any other, except *Defertion*, provided it be without Compulfion or Collufion. But the former may be eafily juftified, both before God and Man.

CASE *the* SECOND, *Resolved.*

IS POLYGAMY, in any Case, lawful under the Gospel?

For *Answer*, it is to be *considered*, that *Marriage* is a *Contract* founded upon the *Laws of Nature*, its *End* being the *Propagation of Mankind*; and the Formality of doing it by Churchmen, is only a supervenient Benediction, or pompous solemnizing of it; and therefore the *Nature of Marriage*, and not any *Forms* used in the *Celebration* of it, is to be *considered*. It is true, the Case is harder when any is married by such a *Form* as binds him to ONE *Woman*, than where he is bound only by the *Tie of Marriage* conceived in *general Terms*.

The Case of Mankind, since the Fall, varies very much from what it was in Innocency; for then the *Soundness* of their *Bodies*, and *Purity* of their *Minds*, did keep out of the Way all the Hazards of Barrenness, Sickness, Uncleanness, or Crossness of Humour; and therefore a single Marriage, as being the perfectest Coalition of Friendship and Interest, was proper to that State; and so *God* made but *one* Woman for *one* Man: But upon the Fall, the Case varied hugely; and Frigidity, Barrenness, Unchastity, Crossness

of

of Humours, made the former Law not so
proper for the following Race of Mankind;
yet still a single Marriage was the perfecter,
as being nearer the Original.

Before the Flood, we find *Lamech* a Po-
LYGAMIST; such were *Abraham* and *Jacob*
after it: So that this was not indulged by
Moses; for all that he did relating to this,
was only to allow a DIVORCE, which was a
Proviso for the Hardness of the *Israelites*
Hearts: Every Man was bound to maintain
whom he had *once* married; lest therefore
such as designed *another* Wife, and could not
maintain the *former*, might use *indirect* Ways
to be rid of them; this *fair one*, of *Divorce*,
was allowed of by God; and this *Polygamy*
was practised, without either Allowance or
Controul, as the natural Right of Mankind;
neither is it any where marked among the
Blemishes of the Patriarchs; *David's* Wives
(and Store of them he had) are termed by
the Prophet, *God's Gift to him:* Yea, *Polygamy* was made, in some Cases, a *Duty* by *Moses's* Law; when any died without Issue, his
Brother, or nearest Kinsman, was to marry
his Wife, for *raising up Seed* to him; and all
were obliged to *obey* this, under the *Hazard*
of the *Infamy* if they *refused* it; neither is
there any Exceptions made for such as were
married; from whence I may faithfully conclude,

de. that what God made needful in some
... to any Degree, can in no wise be
... in it self, since 'twas a Help in ... his
...ys: And thus far, it appears, that Poly-
...ry is not contrary to the Law and Na-
... of *Marriage*. But it is not to be exam...
..., if it is *forbidden* under the Gospel. It is
...tain our *Lord* designed to raise Mankind
...the highest Degrees of Peace and Chastity.
...therefore our *Lord* and St. *Paul* do pre...
... a *single Life* to a married state, as that
...ich qualifies us for the Kingdom of Hea-
..., and was loaded with the fewest Inconve-
...ces; and by this Rule a *single Marriage*
...ng next to none at all, is certainly most
...able to the *Gospel*, and a *single state* or
... *Deluding of Polygamy*, is to be ...
...found. It is true, our *Lord* is repre...
... ... *Code of Poverty*,
...ing, that whosoever puts away his Wife
...and any other becomes commits *Adultery*,
... ... and he that ... with one that
... ... commit *Adultery against* ...
... ... commit
... ... *Wedlock* in need &c. Moreo...
... ... another Woman
... ... and every Man
... V ... ... the ...
... ...
... ...
... ...

feems convincing; yet it will not be found of Weight: For it is to be confidered, that if our *Lord* had been to antiquate POLYGA-MY, it being fo deeply rooted in the Men of that Age, confirmed by fuch famous and un-queftioned Precedents, and riveted by fo long a Practice, he muft have done it plainly and authoritatively; and not in fuch an involved Manner, that it muft be fought out of his Words by the fearch of Logick; neither are thefe dark Words made more clear by any of the *Apoftles* in their Writings. Words are to be carried no farther than the Defign upon which they were written will lead them to; fo that our *Lord* being in that Place to ftrike out *Divorces* fo explicitly, we muft not, by a Confequence, condemn POLYGAMY, fince it feems not to have fallen within the Scope of what our *Lord* does there difapprove: Befides, the Term *Adultery* may be taken in general for fuch a Breach of Wedlock, as is equivalent to *Adultery*; and fuch is *an unjuft Divorce*. This may be the Importance of the Phrafe ufed by *St. Mark*, viz. *He com-mitteth Adultery againft her*; or all may be better explained by the Phrafe *St. Matthew* ufes about it in one Place, *He caufes her to commit Adultery*: Since he that expofeth and tempteth to Sin, fhares in the Guilt with the Perfon that fuccumbs: And from this it appears, that POLYGAMY is not declared

Adultery,

Adultery, neither in the Place cited, nor any other that I know of. But it is true, that POLYGAMY falls short of the Intendment of *Marriage* in Innocency, to which State we that are under the *Gospel*, must return as near as it is possible. It is to be confessed, that POLYGAMY was much condemned by the Ancients: Tho' I think I have met with something about it that is little noticed ; but of *that*, I can adventure to say nothing at this Distance from my Books and Papers. But all That being granted, it is to be considered, that the Ancients were unjust and severe against *Marriage*, and did excessively favour the *Celibate*, or *Single* ; so that in some Places, they who *married* the *second Time*, were put to do *Penance* for it : And, indeed, both *Jew* and *Gentile* had run into such Excess, by their free Commixtures, that it is no Wonder, that if the Holy Men of those Ages, being provoked to a *just* Zeal against such *unjust* Practices, must have been carried through immoderate Swaying of the Counterpoise, into some Extreams on the other Hand : Therefore to conclude this short Answer, wherein many Things are hinted, which might have been enlarged to a Volume, I see nothing so strong *against* POLYGAMY, as to balance the great and visible imminent Hazards, that hang over so many Thousands, if it be not *Allowed.*

NUMBER III.

Two LETTERS *from her Royal Highness the Princess* SOPHIA, *to* JOHN MACKY, *Esq;*

LETTRE I.

LUTZ'BURG, le 16 d'8bre, 1703.

J'Ai receue, Monsieur, *votre obligeante Lettre avec beaucoup de Satisfaction, de voir que voulez bien m'asseurer que l'Affection que vous avez eu pour votre defunt Roy & Maitre, apres la Reyne que vous servez à present, va jusque moi & a mes Descendants. Je suis bien fachée de n'avoir pas été moi meme à* Hanover, *pour vous y voir, & pour vous temoigner combien j'e suis sensible ; car on peut mieux parler qu'ecrire sur tout & que vous me mandez. Cependant vous*

*vous devez croire, que je souhaite les Occasions
de vous en temoigner ma Reconnoisance, & combien je suis,*

Votre tres Affectionée,

SOPHIE Electrice.

LETTER I.

Lutz'burgh, * *Oct.* 16. 1703.

SIR,

I Received your obliging Letter with a
great deal of Satisfaction, to see that you
are pleased to assure me that the *Affection*
which You had for Your late *King* and Master,
after the *Queen* whom You at present serve,
reaches to me and my Heirs. I am very sorry
I was not at *Hanover* my self, to have seen
You, and expressed how *sensible I am of it*;
for it is better to Talk, than Write, on all that
You inform me of. Yet I would have You
to believe, that I wish for Occasions of shew-
ing my Acknowledgment of it, and how much
I am,   Your very Affectionate,

SOPHIA Electress.

* *Lutzelburg :* Or *Lutzburg,* the PALACE her *most
Serene Highness* was then at, is one of *Those* belonging to
the King of *Prussia,* about a League from *Berlin.*

C 2   LET-

N U M B E R IV.

L E T T R E II.

A Hanover le 27ᵐᵉ de Juillet 1706.

MONSIEUR,

JE recois comme un Sureroit d'Obligation les nouvelles Preuves, que vous me donnés de votre zéle, par les Offres de Services que vous me faites au sujet de votre Envoy vers le Païs-Bas Espagnol pour le Retablissement du Negoce & du Commerce des Lettres entre l'Angleterre & ces Provinces. Je vous asseure que j'aurai la Memoire recente de vos honétetès & que je les reconnoîtrai dans les occasions, en vous donnant de veritables Marques de la Consideration particuliere que j'ai pour vous étant toûjours

Votre tres affectionnee

SOPHIE *Electrice.*

LETTER II.

Hanover July 27, 1706.

SIR,

I Efteem as an additional Obligation, the frefh Proofs You give me of Your Zeal, in the Offers of Service you make me with relation to your Commiffion to the *Spanifh-Netherlands,* in order to re-eftablifh a Trade and Correfpondence by Letters betwixt *England* and thofe Provinces. I affure You I fhall always remember Your Civilities, and acknowledge them on all Occafions, by giving You real Marks of the particular Regard I have for You, being always

Your very affectionate,

SOPHIA Electrefs.

C 3 CON-

CONTENTS

OF THE

CHARACTERS of the COURT of GREAT BRITAIN.

Charles,

Table of Contents.

Richard,

Table of CONTENTS,

James,

Table of CONTENTS.

Charles

Table of Contents.

CHARACTERS of the *English* FOREIGN MINISTERS.

Table of CONTENTS.

CHARACTERS of the Officers Military and Naval.

CHA-

Table of CONTENTS.

CHARACTERS of the NOBILITY of SCOTLAND.

Ear

Table of Contents.

An

Table of Contents

An APPENDIX of *Original Papers.*

ERRATA.

PAG. 14. *In the* Note, *dele* late P 95. Read Reprefentative of the *Berties.* P. 130. *Line* 5. *read* Poft-Mafter General. P. 197. for *Carrs,* read *Kers.*

FINIS.

ND - #0122 - 270125 - C0 - 229/152/18 - PB - 9781527738805 - Gloss Lamination